BOATS OF BENGAL

EIGHTEENTH CENTURY PORTRAITS
BY BALTHAZAR SOLVYNS

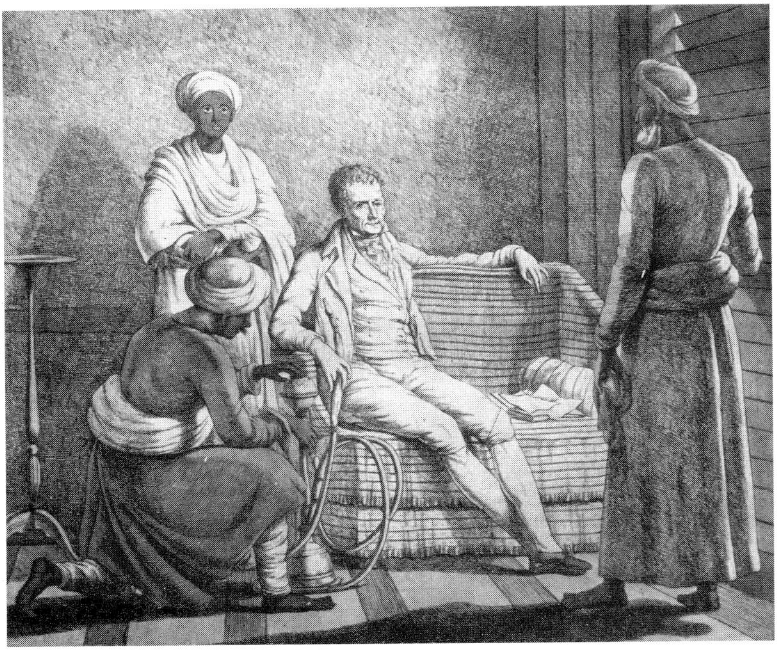

F. Balthazar Solvyns in Calcutta.
Self-Portrait, *Les Hindoûs,* Vol. IV, 1812.

Boats of Bengal

EIGHTEENTH CENTURY PORTRAITS BY BALTHAZAR SOLVYNS

ROBERT L. HARDGRAVE, JR.

MANOHAR
2001

First published 2001

ISBN 81-7304-358-2

Published by
Ajay Kumar Jain for
Manohar Publishers & Distributors
4753/23 Ansari Road, Daryaganj
New Delhi 110002

Typeset by
A J Software Publishing Co. Pvt. Ltd.
305 Durga Chambers
1333 D.B. Gupta Road
Karol Bagh, New Delhi 110005

Printed at
Lordson Publishers Pvt. Ltd.
C 5/19 Rana Pratap Bagh
Delhi-110007

Contents

Acknowledgments

Over the course of my research on Balthazar Solvyns, I have been grateful to a great many people for their assistance in ferreting out elusive information, resolving anomalies, and in finding the correct Bengali, Hindustani, or Persian word for what in Solvyns's description was by no means always clear. Specifically, in my work on Solvyns's portrayals of the boats of Bengal, I want to express my thanks to Anne Bulley, South Chard, Somerset; Daniel Finamore, Curator of Maritime Arts and History, Peabody Essex Museum, Salem, Massachusetts; and Anand Yang, Professor of History, the University of Utah, Salt Lake City. For assistance in Bengali transliteration, I would like to thank Aditi Sen, American Institute of Indian Studies, Calcutta, and Sagaree Sengupta, South Asian Studies, the University of Wisconsin at Madison.

Thanks go as well to the American Institute of Indian Studies and to the University Research Institute of the University of Texas at Austin for support in the larger Solvyns project.

The University of Texas at Austin — ROBERT L. HARDGRAVE, JR.
August 1999

Introduction: F. Balthazar Solvyns

The Boats of Bengal is part of a larger project on the life and work of the Flemish artist François Balthazar Solvyns, whose portrayal of the people and culture of Bengal is among the richest visual records we have of India in the late eighteenth century.[1]

Solvyns was born in Antwerp in 1760, the youngest child of a family of properous merchants. Growing up in a city with the rich artistic tradition of Rubens, Jordeans, and Van Dyck, the young Solvyns began the study of art at Antwerp's Académie des Beaux-Arts, where in 1772, he received the first prize in drawing. At the Académie, he pursued studies in the new Neo-classical curriculum. In 1778, Solvyns went to Paris to become the pupil of François-André Vincent (1746-1816), one of the major figures of the Neo-classical movement. While in Paris, Solvyns came to know the work of the French marine painter Claude Joseph Vernet (1714-1789), who had been commissioned by Louis XV to paint a series of the ports of France.

Whether influenced by Vernet or by exposure to the tradition of marine painting in the Low Countries, Solvyns, on his return to Antwerp, soon embarked upon a career as a marine painter. In 1780, when only 20 years old, he accepted a commission from the Governor-General of the Austrian Netherlands to paint the port of Ostend. Solvyns now on his way to becoming the "Belgium Vernet" soon secured another commission to paint the port of Antwerp. Both the Ostend and Antwerp paintings were hung in the Laeken palace, outside Brussels, where Solvyns had accepted a post on appointment by his new patrons, the Archduchess Marie-Christina and her husband Albert, the Governors-General. In 1789, at the time of the Brabant revolution, Marie-Christina and Albert fled to Vienna, taking the paintings with them. The Ostend painting is known to have been in the Albertina palace in Vienna until 1919, but it along with the Antwerp painting are now lost, and the Ostend work survives only as a print, "*View of the City and Port of Ostend,*" engraved by Robert Daudet (1737-1824) after the Solvyns painting, and published in Paris in 1784.[2]

There are records of other marine paintings from the 1780s by Solvyns. In 1789, he joined a group of artists for a public exhibition in Antwerp, showing three oil paintings and a drawing—all marine subjects. The whereabouts of these pictures—or whether they have survived—is today unknown. Indeed, the only Solvyns painting known to survive from this period is "*The View of a Dutch Port*," signed and dated 1787, in Antwerp's National Maritime Museum.[3]

There are few accounts of Solvyns's life, and the earliest, published soon after his death in 1824, contains inaccuracies that were repeated in subsequent entries in various biographical dictionaries. Among the most glaring of these errors and anomalies is the report that Solvyns fled in 1789 with his patron Marie-Christina to Vienna and remained there until her death, after which he sailed to India. Another oft-repeated mistake has Solvyns, in sailing with Home Popham, making charts of the Red Sea. What we do know is that during the political unrest in the Low Countries in 1789-1790 and without his former patronage, Solvyns, at the age of 30, made the decision to go to India to seek his fortune.

The voyage to India usually took some four to eight months, depending upon the time of year, prevailing trade winds, and possible mishaps—with the return voyage typically taking somewhat longer. Solvyns set sail from Ostend in July 1790 aboard the *Etrusco*, owned and under the command of Captain Home Popham.[4] He arrived in Calcutta eight months later, in March 1791.

During the twelve years that Solvyns lived in Calcutta, he struggled to find his place as an artist and a position in society. He found success in neither. Commissions were not forthcoming, and he was compelled to offer his services in teaching painting, restoring pictures, and—for Stuart & Co., Coachmakers—decorating coaches and palanquins. He did, however, secure commissions for several paintings, and among those surviving—or known—are the six marine paintings.[5] Three (each oil on panel) are in museums: "*The Charlotte of Chittagong*," 1792, in the National Maritime Museum, Greenwich;[6] "*Unidentified British East Indiaman at Calcutta*," 1794,[7] and "*The Launching of Gabriel Gillett's Armed Merchantman in Calcutta Harbor*," c. 1798,[8] both in the Peabody Essex Museum, Salem, Massachusetts. The "*Launching*" portrays the ship and the rich life of the Calcutta docks, with Solvyns himself standing with his sketchbook.

Other Solvyns marine paintings done in India are with dealers or in private collections. "*Calcutta From Below Fort William Looking*

North,"[9] an unsigned oil on canvas and attributed to Solvyns, is a smaller version of a painting, signed and dated 1792, which was damaged and subsequently destroyed. "*The Marquis Cornwallis,*" 1793 (oil on panel), was probably commissioned by the ship's builders. The ship went on to become famous in the history of Australia. After its construction in Calcutta, the ship went to Cork, Ireland, and from there transported Irish political prisoners to Australia in 1795, only to confront mutiny on the voyage. The painting came onto the market from a private collection in the 1990s with the sale of the ship's log. At least one other Solvyns marine painting remains in a private collection.

Despite his prominent Antwerp family background, Solvyns—a foreigner—remained marginal to British society in Calcutta. He was never invited to become a member of the Asiatic Society of Bengal, founded by the great Orientalist Sir William Jones, whom Solvyns so admired. Indeed, the records of the Society for the period of Solvyns's residence in Calcutta indicate that he never even once attended its meetings. Moreover, Solvyns—always burdened by financial pressure—lived on the margin of the European quarter, in the area of old central Calcutta that abutted the native quarter, "Black Town," to the north. His very "marginality," both socially and physically, may have been critical in opening up the artist to the experience of India around him, but Solvyns was naturally curious and, as an artist, acutely observant. His own exclusion from the elite European circles in which he would have loved to move, however, may well have deepened his sympathy for India and for Indians.

Solvyns's genuine interest in the people around him was reinforced by an intellectual background in the Enlightenment. He brought its "*Histoire naturelle*" perspective and commitment to truth to the project that was to consume his life—a portrayal of the Hindus.

In 1794, Solvyns placed an advertisement in the *Calcutta Gazette,*[10] announcing his intention to publish "*A Collection of Two Hundred and Fifty Coloured Etchings Descriptive of the Manners, Customs, and Dresses of the Hindoos.*" It was the most ambitious publishing venture yet undertaken in India. The collection was published in Calcutta in a few copies in 1796, and then in greater numbers in 1799. Divided into twelve parts, the first section, with 66 prints, depicts "the Hindoo Casts, with their professions." Following sections portray servants, costumes, means of transportation (carts, palanquins, and boats), modes of smoking, fakirs, musical instruments,[11] and festivals. Solvyns portrays the boats of Bengal in two sections, Section VIII, "*Pleasure Boats,*" and Section IX, "*Boats and Vessels of Burden.*"

The Calcutta prints have compelling immediacy and constitute a rich visual account of the people of Bengal in the late eighteenth century, but the etchings, by European standards of the time, were considered "rough" and "crude," and they did not appeal to the vogue of the picturesque. For all Solvyns's effort, the project proved a financial failure. In 1803, he left India for Europe, and soon redid the etchings for a folio edition of 288 plates, *Les Hindoûs,* published in Paris between 1808 and 1812 in four volumes.

In his introduction to the first volume, Solvyns writes that although European scholars have done much "to dispel the darkness which enveloped the geography and history of India, . . . its inhabitants alone have not yet been observed nor represented with the accuracy which is necessary to make them perfectly known. . . ." To rectify this situation, he offered to the public *Les Hindoûs,* "the result of a long and uninterrupted study of this celebrated nation."

> The drawings from which are engraved the numerous plates . . . were taken by myself upon the spot. Instead of trusting to the words of others, or remaining satisfied with the knowledge contained in preceding authors, I have spared neither time, nor pains, nor expense, to see and examine with my own eyes, and to delineate every object with the most minute accuracy . . . .
>
> I admitted nothing as certain but upon the proof of my own observation, or upon such testimony as I knew to be incontrovertible. I have wholly neglected the testimony of authors who have treated these subjects before me, and have given only what I have seen, or what I have myself heard from the mouth of the natives the best informed and most capable of giving me true instructions upon the subject of my inquiries.[12]

Les Hindoûs was lavishly published, and each colored etching was accompanied by a descriptive text, in both French and English. The Institut de France accepted the dedication of the work, observing "as a particular merit, the character of faithfulness to local detail that is lacking in almost all engravings of picturesque travels."[13] But even these sumptuous volumes failed commercially, victim to the unrest of the Napoleonic wars, to a changing taste that relegated Solvyns to the past, and to their staggeringly high price. When the Kingdom of the Netherlands was formed in 1814, Solvyns returned to his native Antwerp, where he was appointed Captain of the Port, a position bestowed by William I in recognition of his accomplishments as an artist. Solvyns's last great work—and his largest painting—portrays the arrival of the king by sea to the port of Antwerp. In the picture, Solvyns includes himself, standing in a small boat, greeting the royal yacht.[14] François Balthazar Solvyns died in Antwerp in 1824.

Solvyns's portrayal of the Hindus, with its accompanying descriptions, constitutes the first "ethnographic survey" of India or, more properly, of Bengal. Yet this contribution has never been recognized, and historians or anthropologists have rarely drawn upon Solvyns for an understanding of society in India in the late eighteenth century. As a marine painter, Solvyns brought a special interest to the ships and "country boats" of India, and with knowledge of naval architecture and a trained eye, he provides an unparalleled portrayal of the boats of Bengal.

NOTES

1 On Solvyns, see Hardgrave, "A Portrait of Black Town: Baltazard Solvyns in Calcutta, 1791-1804," and Hardgrave and Slawek, "Introduction," 1-11. In the course of my research on Solvyns, new materials have necessarily brought some revisions to my earlier discussion of his life, as in the date of Solvyns's departure from India. Solvyns is included in a list of European residents in Calcutta in 1804, but it is almost certain that he sailed from India in 1803, for he was again in Europe in 1804, and he married Marie Anne Greenwood in Brussels in November of that year. Solvyns used his middle name, but spelled it variously—"Baltazard" on the title pages of *Les Hindoûs*, the Paris edition of his etchings, but more usually as "Balthazar," as he was baptised and as his wife gave his name in the announcement of his death. Hardgrave, *A Portrait of the Hindus: Balthazar Solvyns Life and Work*, now in preparation, will reproduce the complete collection of the Solvyns etchings, with annotations and introductory chapters on the artist's life and work.

On Solvyns, also see Archer, "Baltazard Solvyns and the Indian Picturesque," and Archer and Archer, "Francois Baltazard Solvyns: Early Painter of Calcutta Life."

2 Copies of the Daudet engraving, "*Vue de la Ville et du Port d'Ostende*" (37.5 x 58 cm), are in the Stadsarchief, Ostend (V.373), and in the Cabinet des estampes, Bibliothèque royale Albert I, Brussels (S.II. 40651). It is reproduced in Hosten, "De zee en de kunst," 47; Hosten, "Frans-Balthasar Solvyns," 19; and Hosten, "Omtrent een Gezicht op de Haven van de Stad Oostende," 117.

3 The painting, oil on panel, Nationaal Sheepaartmuseum, Het Steen,

Antwerp, is reproduced in Woussen, 304; Hosten, "Solvyns, François-Balthazar," 153; and Hosten, "Schilders van e zee."

4 On Home Popham (1762-1820), see the biography by his descendant Hugh Popham and the entry in *The Dictionary of National Bibliography*, 16:143-46.

5 All the known Solvyns paintings will be discussed in detail and reproduced in Hardgrave, *A Portrait of the Hindus* (forthcoming).

6 The painting is reproduced in Kemp and Ormond, Pl. 59, and in the National Maritime Museum, *Concise Catalog*, p. 368; in Archibald, Pl. XXII; and in Hosten, "Solvyns, François-Balthazar," 151.

7 Reproduced in Smith, 67; Berko and Berko, 8-9; and Hosten, "Schilders van e zee."

8 Reproduced on the cover of *The American Neptune: Maritime History & Arts* (55, Winter 1995), published by the Peabody Essex Museum, Salem, Massachusetts.

9 Reproduced in Spink & Son, *A Journey Through India: Pictures of India by British Artists*, catalogue for the sale, October 9-November 1, 1996, Pl. 36, p. 38. Unsold, the painting was offered for sale at auction by Christies, "Visions of India," in October 1999. The larger, 1792 painting, "Men of War and Other Craft of Calcutta," was illustrated in the advertisement by Spink & Co. in *The Burlington Magazine* (March 1950).

10 February 6, 1794 (Vol. 20, No. 519), 2, reprinted in Seton-Karr, 2:575-77.

11 Solvyns's etchings of musical instruments are illustrated and discussed in Hardgrave and Slawek.

12 Solvyns, *Les Hindoûs*, 1:20-21.

13 Solvyns quotes the letter from the Institut's Secretary in its entirely in his January 1, 1812, "Prospectus" for *Les Hindoûs*.

14 The painting, oil on canvas, is with the Australian branch of the Solvyns family, descendants of Balthazar's brother Laurent-Maximilien. Balthazar Solvyns and his wife Marie Anne had three children, but no surviving grandchildren.

Boats of Bengal

There are a great variety of distinctive boats in Bengal and many variations of the same type, reflecting local traditions, adaptations to navigational requirements, and user demands. Moreover, "the same name might often designate different boats and, conversely, a single type of boat might be referred to in different areas by different names."[1] "Different names can also be given to the same boat to give expression to the purpose for which it is used."[2] Solvyns's names for the various boats generally conform to Anglo-Indian usage, but in some instances, his ear may have failed him or he mistook for a name an informant's response to his question as to what kind of boat it is.

In its riverine character, Bengal in Solvyns's time afforded little use of carriages or carts beyond Calcutta. "Almost all journeys are by boat," Grandpré wrote of his travels in 1789-1790. "Bengal is so intersected with rivers and canals that you can go to any part of it in a boat."[3]

Boats were also for pleasure and provided a refreshing alternative to an evening carriage ride over Calcutta's dusty roads, but a boating expedition on the Hugli River, say to suburban Garden Reach, for all the charm of its elegant country houses and cool breezes, might well meet with "unsavory smells and the sight of animal or even human carcasses on the banks."[4] Wealthy Europeans and opulent Hindus kept their own, often richly ornamented, boats—pinnaces (Pl. 2), bājrās (Pl. 5), and magnificent "snake boats" (Pls. 3 and 4). For these outings, crews were handsomely dressed, and the passengers entertained by musicians.

Among the boats portrayed by Solvyns are those that carry cargo or passengers for longer river voyages. These "Ganges boats" are "generally broad in beam to avoid awkward squalls, and draw little water so as to escape the numerous shoals."[5] Indeed, flat-bottomed boats are still widely used in Bengal because of the many sandbars in the rivers.

Depending on the depth of water, currents, and weather

conditions, boatmen row, paddle, pole, and tow their boats, and, with favorable winds, raise the sail. Colesworthy Grant, in *Rural Life in Bengal,* writes that most "Indian boats, though built, adapted, and provided for rowing, are *sailing* boats; and being round, or flat at the bottom, having no keels, are of course very liable, if caught in a squall, or through carelessness falling into the trough of rough water, to be overturned. Hence, in a great measure, the frightful extent of casualties on the river during some of our sudden squalls or terrible nor'-west gales."[6]

Many of Solvyns's boats are portrayed without a mast, though in the text there is reference to sail. The masts may be taken down and are frequently shown in the etchings laid horizontally, usually from the support to which it is hinged.[7] To raise the mast, it is "stepped" into a box-like support (called a "tabernacle") in which the heel of the mast is fixed.

Most often, writes William Crooke, "There is a single mast carrying a rude sail, a marvel of rents and patches, of dull brown colour. . . . Going downstream, [the boat] is propelled by a long bamboo pole, and guided by a large rudder of the most clumsy construction." But going upriver, boats such as the bājrā, must usually be tracked "by ropes fastened to the top of the mast, and each tracker has a separate rope, so that the watchful eye of the skipper may detect if any man is shirking in his work."[8]

In a number of the etchings, Solvyns follows the convention among marine artists of portraying the boat broadside in the center foreground with (or, alternatively, without) the mast set, while the same boat is depicted in the background in a stern and/or bow view and/or at a different point of sail. Thus, for example, when Solvyns portrays the pānsi (Pl. 9) with mast down, in the background, the boat is shown with the mast stepped and sail unfurled.

Historian Radha Kumud Mookerji concludes his 1912 study of Indian shipping with reference to Solvyns's "very interesting account, together with very fine sketches, of the typical Indian (Hindu) ships that were in use in the earlier part of the 19th century." He then quotes selectively from Solvyns's descriptions of various boats, illustrating the vessels with seven drawings made after Solvyns's etchings. In a footnote, he writes of *Les Hindoûs,* "This rare work is to be found in the splendid library of Mr. Abanindranath Tagore, the renowned Bengali artist. . . ."[9]

In the Calcutta edition of the etchings, Solvyns divided his portrayal of boats into two sections—Section XIII, 13 prints of "pleasure boats," and Section XIV, 17 prints of "boats and vessels of burden." Two additional prints depicting boats, the Bore and the Northwester, precede Sections VIII and IX. In the 1799 *Catalogue,* he writes:

> The different kinds of boats of Hindostan are admirably adapted to the navigation of the various parts in which they are used;—the rivers of the northern provinces require flat broad vessels, with little draft of water; while the southern navigation admits of a construction of greater depth, for security against the high waves of the larger branches of the Berampoter [Brahmaputra] and Ganges.[10]

For the Paris edition, *Les Hindoûs,* Vol. III, Solvyns presents the boats in six sections (or "numbers," as he terms them), each beginning with a large, double-sized etching. In his Introduction, he assures the reader that his portrayals are based on his own observations and with concern for "truth and exactness of detail." This is surely true for the thirty-two etchings appearing in the Calcutta edition, for which the original drawings exist. The four etchings in the Paris edition that were not included in the earlier collection are problematic, particularly the two etchings that bring several ships together in composite portrayals, *View of Ballasore Roads* (Pl. 19) and *Vessels of all Sorts* (Pl. 36). Here, at least with respect to some of the ships portrayed, Solvyns appears to have copied another artist's print or painting to illustrate a particular kind of vessel.

The Introduction to the third volume of *Les Hindoûs* lays out the plan for the presentation of the prints. Thirty-six etchings portray boats of Bengal, the number, in Solvyns's judgment, "necessary to give a competent idea of their [the Hindus'] navigation."

> Many travellers have bestowed general praises upon the naval arts of the Hindoos, but as none of them have entered into any detail, the subject notwithstanding their elogiums, remained unknown in Europe. This may be deemed therefore the first attempt which has been made, to give a complete description of all the different vessels used in those countries.
>
> My taste as well as my reflections, led me to give a particular attention to this subject, and I believe that my drawings are not liable to any reproach, with respect to their truth and exactness of detail. The multitude of vessels which fill the six first numbers of this volume, may at first sight occasion some surprise, but we must consider, that the greater part of them are meer boats;

and it is natural enough that the Hindoos being debarred from maritime expeditions by their religion, which enjoins them not to quit their country, should turn all their attention to inland navigation, and bring it to as great a degree of perfection as the genious of their nation could attain, to which a free scope was given, by the great number of navigable rivers by which Hindoostan is traversed, whose annual inundations, force the neighbouring inhabitants to have recourse to this mode of communication. Hence that variety of boats and barges for the purposes of pleasure or commerce. The first offer an easy and expeditious mode of travelling; by the second, the communications between the country and great towns are kept up, and the wants of their vast population supplied. The forms of both are decided by the local circumstances: in the north of Hindoostan for example, where the waters are subject to little agitation, they are generally flat bottomed; while near the coast, on the contrary they have sharp keels, to resist and cut the waves. Though not a single nail of iron enters into their structure, it is exceedingly solid. This manner of building boats without iron, is very ancient in India. Procopius[11] takes notice of it in his history of the Persian wars, and says that it was known also to the Ethiopians. The engravings in the six first numbers, represent faithfully the forms of all these vessels, and the text enters into every detail of their construction and use, as well as the advantages and disadvantages which attend them. I have sometimes had recourse to a larger scale, to give a clearer idea of the manner of adapting and managing the oars, and of some of the minuter parts of the tackle. I think it necessary to repeat here my assertion, that I never on any occasion whatsoever exceed the bounds of my own observations, which may quit the doubts of those readers, who are always ready to suspect the veracity of a traveller when he relates customs in opposition to those received in Europe, or ventures to contradict what has been related by other respectable travellers. In this manner doubts have been entertained about what I have said of the Pariahs; founded upon their opposition to the prior reports of other creditable authors. I am nevertheless obliged to repeat what I advanced in the first volume, that there never existed in India a particular caste of Pariahs,[12] that the word is generally applied to all that is mean, bad and contemptable; so that my subject may naturally lead me to speak perhaps of a Pariah ship, a term familiar to every sailor who has frequented the Indian seas.

The larger ingravings of the six first numbers of this volume, relate more or less to the navigation of Hindoostan: the two first represents a phenomena well known and dreaded by Indian mariners, the North Wester [Pl. 1] and the Maerce [*macreé*, or bore, Pl. 7]. I have endeavoured to retrace their effects with as much truth as such a subject will admit, where the fury of the sea and of the heavens are combined in all their horror. The text will furnish a minute description of these singular phenomena, which appear with more or less violence on all the coasts of India, and not without reason struck

Alexander with astonishment as he entered the mouth of the Indus. The third large print [Pl. 13] is a view of the island of Penang, much frequented by the Indian and Malayan shipping; especially the latter, which renders this island interesting, by affording an opportunity of comparing the naval craft of these two nations; and to give the reader an opportunity of carrying these comparisons still further, I have brought together in the sixth print of the last number [Pl. 36], all the different species of shipping, which are habitually seen in the Indian seas.

The fourth large print of this volume [Pl. 19], represents the road of Balasore, in which is the principal entrance of the river Ougly [Hugli], and where a number of vessels constantly stop, some to take in, others to discharge their pilots

The fifth large engraving [Gudārā, Pl. 25], represents the manner of passing the Ganges. . . .[13]

A Note on the Solvyns Plates and Text and on the Annotations

The plates for *Boats of Bengal* are from *Les Hindoûs*, Vol. III, published in Paris in 1811. In the Paris edition, as noted above, the first etching in each section of six is a large, double-plate. In the portrayal of boats, there are six double-plates (Pls. 1, 7, 13, 19, 25, and 36). The regular etchings measure 34.5 x 24 cm; the double-plates, 34.5 x 48 cm. In portraying Solvyns's boats in this volume, I have included one etching from the Calcutta edition, Bangles (Pl. 21a), both for comparison of the Calcutta and Paris etchings and because of the notable difference between the two in Solvyns's depiction of the boat. The Calcutta etchings, as the one here, measure 37 x 25 cm.

For each plate, I include the descriptive text from Solvyns's *A Catalogue of 250 Coloured Etchings; Descriptive of the Manners, Customs, Characters, Dress, and Religious Ceremonies of the Hindoos*, published in Calcutta in 1799 to accompany the collection of etchings,[14] as well as Solvyns's more detailed text for the Paris edition, *Les Hindoûs*. The English text in *Les Hindoûs* accompanying Solvyns's portraits of the boats is reproduced as it appears in the original. The annotations clarify and elaborate Solvyns's text and direct the reader to relevant literature. Footnotes for the text and annotations for the Solvyns portraits use shortened references to the sources cited, referring the reader to the bibliography.

Solvyns's original drawings for the etchings are in the Victoria and

Albert Museum, London.[15] Each is accompanied by a hand-written description, most of which correspond closely to the text of the 1799 *Catalogue.* Where Solvyns's note to the original drawing provides additional information, I make reference to it in the Commentary.

NOTES

1 Deloche, 2:156, fn. 44. Prinsep, in 1830, in Appendix A4, devotes seven pages to 29 etchings illustrative of his "remarks concerning country boats" of Bengal, 48-49. The variety of boats are portrayed in some 150 color photographs in Jansen, *Sailing Against the Wind.* On the boats of Bengal, see Greenhill and, more particularly, on boat types and construction, Jansen, *The Country Boats of Bangladesh,* 70-105, and Tamonash C. Das Gupta, 13-40. Also see Hornell's discussion of "Boats of the Ganges," in *Water Transport,* 241-53. A compendium of Hindustani terms relating to country boats of Bihar (many similar to those used in Bengal) is included in Grierson, 42-45. Of great scholarly value is Deloche's work on "modes water transport" in India, 2:127-222, which draws on Solvyns's portrayals, with sketches from the etchings to depict various boats of Bengal, 2:156-64.

2 Jansen, *The Country Boats of Bangladesh,* 74.

3 2:17.

4 Suresh Chandra Ghosh, 140.

5 Crooke, *Things Indian,* 428.

6 Grant here refers to "all boats," but later, 26, modifies his sweeping generalization.

7 This is clearly depicted in a photograph in Jansen, *Sailing Against the Wind,* 52-53.

8 *Things Indian,* 428. On tracking, see Deloche, 2:172-74; Greenhill, *Boats and Boatmen of Pakistan,* 45-46; and Bernstein, 16-20. See the description of tracking in the Commentary on the bājrā (Pl. 5).

9 250. The drawings, copies of Solvyns, are inscribed "Seyne." In the preface, x, Mookerji writes, "To the kindness of some of my artist friends I owe the sketches of several representations of ships. . . ."

10 19.

11 Byzantine historian (c.499-565).

12 Solvyns makes this assertion in *Les Hindoûs,* I.2.6. There is surely a "Pariah" (Paraiyan) caste in South India, though in Calcutta, Solvyns would not have encountered it. The term "pariah," however, was widely used among Europeans in India to refer to the worst of almost anything, including "pariah ships."

13 3:1-2. Solvyns's idiosyncratic spellings are retained.

14 Published in octavo (Calcutta: Mirror Press, 1799), the *Catalogue* contains brief descriptions of the etchings, usually no more than a few words or a paragraph at most.

15 "A Collection of Two Hundred and Fifty Drawings Descriptive of the Manners Customs and Dresses of the Hindoos by Balt. Solvyns. Calcutta," Department of Prints and Drawings, Victoria and Albert Museum. Press Mark: S-20 (Reg. No. 8937.1-98; 8937.98a-247). Two drawings are missing and apparently were not in the collection when the museum acquired it in the late nineteenth century.

1. North-Wester

Calcutta: Before Sec. IX. A North-Wester off Calcutta.
Paris: III.1.1. North-Wester.

The phenomenon which I am going to describe borrows its name from the wind by which it is occasioned: it takes place in the gulf of Bengal and the rivers of Hindoostan, more particularly in the south-east monsoon. The print represents a view to the north-west of Calcutta. In the morning a south wind, warmer than usual, reigns upon the river; from sunrise the sky is clear till about noon, when some clouds, which appear to come from the high mountains, meet on the horizon to the north, and soon accumulate so as to cover nearly the whole of the sky: the south wind ceases and a dead calm succeeds for a few minutes. On a sudden this momentary silence of nature is followed by a dreadful noise which seems to announce the confusion of all the elements. The clouds thicken, and are torn by continual flashes of lightning, the thunder roars, and torrents of rain often deluge the country: the atmosphere becomes a few degrees cooler. The river then assumes the appearance of a boisterous sea, and sometimes overwhelms the vessels which have not had the produce to fly for shelter to the creeks or canals. These disasters are but too frequent, and I myself have seen ships at anchor with their topmasts lowered veer round and disappear under the waves: these accidents are often too sudden to be prevented. I shall have occasion frequently, in the course of this volume, to mention again the dismal effects of these periodical tempests.

Commentary: Bengal's North-Wester, or Nor'-wester in Anglo-Indian parlance, is a sudden and violent storm, with winds that may reach more than 100 miles per hour. Arising in the "hot season," April through June, Bengalis call them *kāl baisākī*, "disasters of May." They are typically preceded by a dust storm and followed by hail and as much as 20 inches of rain in a single storm.[1] They are, as Mrs. Kindersley wrote from Calcutta in 1766, "altogether tremendous."[2]

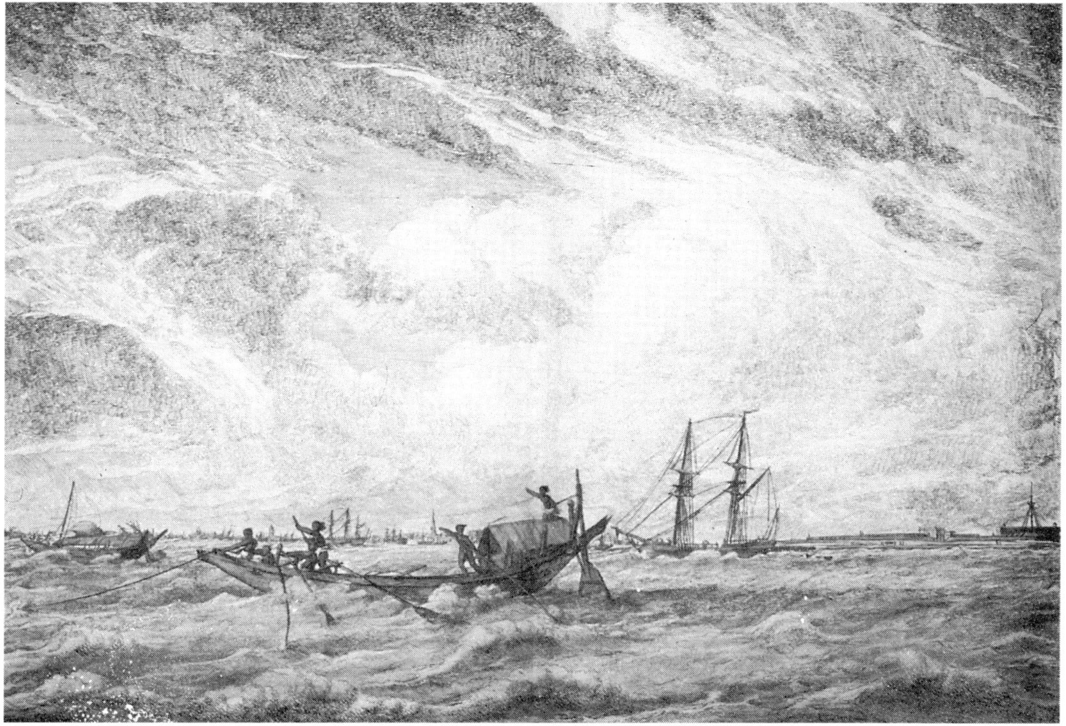

NORTH-WESTER. Paris: III.1.1. (double plate)

Solvyns portrays the North-Wester on the Hugli river with the buildings of Calcutta seen on the distant shore. Oarsmen on a bhur (Pl. 33), center, struggle in the wind.

NOTES

1 Hobson-Jobson, 630, and Greenhill, *Boats and Boatmen of Pakistan.* 24.
2 83.

2. Pinnace

Calcutta: Sec. VIII, No. 1. A Pinnace or Yatch [obs., yacht] for the inland Navigation.
Paris: III.1.2. A Pinnace or Yatch.

These yatchs which are made use of by Europeans are very commodious and generally employed for the voyage from Calcutta to Banares, Lucknow, etc. There are others which belong to private people, and sail down the river to its mouth; but these are real ships and could stand the open sea. I speak here only of the public pinnace. They carry sail, and are generally strongly masted: each one is divided into two or three apartments, one for company, another for the beds, and a third as a cabinet, besides a place called *varandah* forwards for the servants. The yatch has several attendant boats to carry provisions and serve for kitchen and other offices, which keep to leeward not to incommode their masters with the smoke. They have in general as many conveniencies as a small house. The sailors, called *Dandys* [*dāṇḍī*] labour day and night to stem the strongest currents. The assiduity with which these people work is the more surprising, as their wages are very moderate, and their nourishment exceedingly frugal, a little fish and rice, with water. They are continually smoking the *hooka*.

Commentary: The pinnace (*pinās* in Bengali) takes its name from the French word for the long, narrow boat with a sharp stern used in the Bay of Biscay.[1] The boat was introduced in Bengal and was the "largest and handsomest boats" used principally by Europeans.[2] The pinnace is generally schooner-rigged and has two masts, though sometimes one. It is typically 40 to 50 feet in length, with a burden of 12 to 20 tons. Its crew, under a captain, usually called the *mājhī*[3] or *serang*,[4] ranges from 12 to 16 *dāṇḍīs*—or *māllās*, another word for the boatmen—who row, pole, or tug when the wind is insufficient to use the sails.[5] In his note to the original drawing of the pinnace,

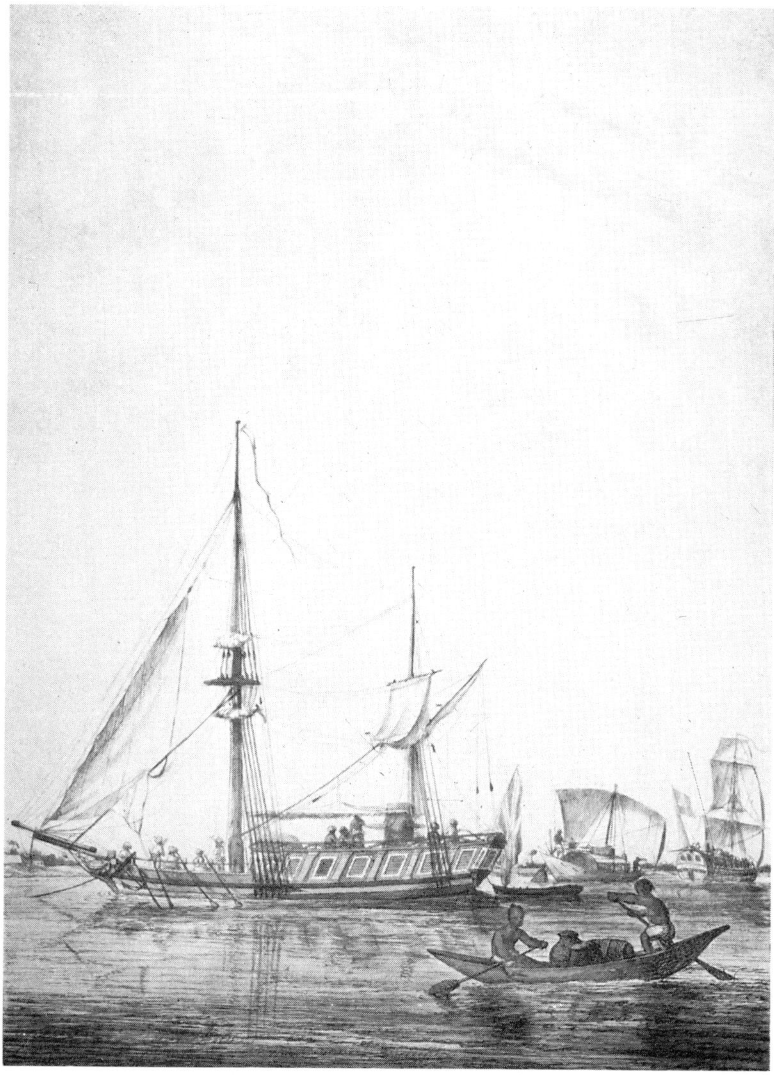

PINNACE. Paris: III.1.2.

Solvyns writes that "they draw little water, and are therefore well calculated for inland navigation."

In Solvyns's time and well into the nineteenth century, the pinnace was used to transfer passengers to Calcutta from Diamond Harbor, 41 miles down river, the usual anchorage for Indiamen, or from Kijari (Kedgeree), 68 miles below Calcutta near the mouth of the Hugli, where the larger ships used to anchor.[6]

Pinnaces were usually owned privately by wealthy officials and merchants, but Governor-General Wellesley had, as the East India Company's state yacht, a pinnace, the "Soonamooky" (having the "appearance of gold"), that Sir Charles D'Oyly depicted in a print.[7] Williamson, in the accompanying text, describes the boat, originally built for Warren Hastings, as "a strong mixture of European and Oriental architecture." Taking about 30 oars, it was constructed "of teak, sheathed with copper, and fitted up in a style suited to the dignity of a Viceroy." In the print, the pinnace is accompanied by a fīlcehrā (Pl. 3).

Pinnaces could be hired in Calcutta for pleasure trips or short journeys, but because they were expensive to hire, they were rarely used for lengthy journeys.[8] They did, however, provide superior accommodation to the more widely used, but cumbersome bājrā (Pl. 5), and, as Tennant noted in 1797, "from its resembling the structure of European craft, both in the hull and rigging, it is better fitted for encountering a gale in the great river."[9]

The pinnace, accompanied by smaller service vessels, was sometimes used by more prosperous Europeans for extended travel up river into the interior. In 1823, Fanny Parks described the boats for a three to four month trip from Calcutta to Lucknow taken by friends: "a very fine sixteen-oared pinnace, containing two excellent cabins, fitted up with glazed and Venetian windows, pankhas [fans], and two shower-baths;" "a dinghee for the cook, and provisions"; an immense baggage boat, containing all their furniture"; "a vessel for the washerman, his wife, and the dogs"; and two large boat with the horses. "What a number of boats for one family!" she declared, "An absolute fleet."[10] The pinnace and its supporting boats could well have a total crew of more than one hundred plus an equal number of servants to attend to the passengers' every need.[11]

About two-thirds of the boat is given to often luxurious accommodation. In the front, several steps down from the fore deck, is an open verandah, as Solvyns describes. This opens into a comfortable living and dining area, behind which are two, sometimes three, spacious cabins, a bathroom and storage closets. The rooms are well-ventilated and cooled by the sway of *pankhās* or by mats that are sprinkled with water over the venetianed windows.[12]

Captain Thomas Williamson, in his *East India Vide-Mecum*, 1810, describes the windows used on both the pinnace and the bājrā: "The sides [of the interior cabins] are furnished, for their whole length, with Venetian blinds, in frames which lift up by means of hinges at their tops; and a long curtain, made either of tarpaulin, or of painted, or of white canvas, is nailed on the outside; letting down at pleasure, to keep out wind, rain, dust, &c."[13]

"The roofs of these boats are usually flat; and some have side rails to prevent luggage, or those who sleep there, from falling overboard. . . . Baggage may be put under the deck; but that part is generally occupied by the dandies, (or rowers,) if permitted to sleep there. . . ."[14]

In the Calcutta edition, the pinnace is portrayed alone, filling the etching. For the Paris edition, Solvyns depicts other boats at sail in the background—a brig (Pl. 26) and what may be a bhur (Pl. 33)—and, in the foreground, two rowers take a ḍiṅgi out with supplies for the pinnace.

NOTES

1 Kerchove, 534. Also see Kemp. In his description of the pinnace, Kemp reproduces Solvyns's Calcutta etching, but makes no reference to the boat in India.

2 Colesworthy Grant, *Rural Life in Bengal*, 4-5, with a small engraving.

3 The *mājhī* (Bengali) is the master or steersman of any native river-craft. The commonly used Anglo-Indian name *mangee* is from the Hindi *mānjhī*. *Hobson-Jobson*, 558.

4 Boatswain or skipper of a small native vessel; from the Persian *sarhang*, overseer. *Hobson-Jobson*, 812.

5 Hunter, *A Statistical Account of Bengal*, 1:33; Grant and Colebrooke, 116-17. Solvyns portrays the *dānḍī* (Calcutta: Sec. I., No. 45; Paris: I.9.5). The *dānḍī* is a boatman or oarsman peculiar to the Gangetic rivers. The word is derived from the Arabic *dānḍ*, "staff, oar." *Hobson-Jobson*, 288: Lewis 98. Captain Thomas Williamson, 283-88, in *The East India Vide-Mecum*, details the work of the *dānḍī* as an oarsman or rower, and he provides the descriptive text to D'Oyly's portrayal of Marquis Wellesley's *dānḍī* in *The European in India* (Pl. 12). *Dānḍīs* are discussed in the Commentary on the Bājrā (Pl. 5).

A common Anglo-Indian word for the native sailor was *lascar.* Solvyns portrays the Clashy in *Les Hindoûs,* IV.3.6.

6 See Commentaries for Balasore Roads (Pl. 19) and Sloop (Pl. 31).

7 "Marquis Wellesley's Dandy, or Boatman, in his Livery," Pl. 12, *The European in India.*

8 Grant, *Rural Life in Bengal,* 4.

9 1:46-47.

10 1:31.

11 *Admiral Paris' Native Boats,* 34-35.

12 Ibid. For descriptions, see also Lawrence, 51, reprinted in Nair, *Calcutta in the 19th Century,* 616, and London Missionary, *Travels in India* (1852), in Nair, *Calcutta in the 19th Century,* 948.

13 1:129-30.

14 Ibid.

3. Fīlcehrā

Calcutta: Sec. VIII, No. 2. A Feal Chara, named from the elephant's head;— used by the Princes and Nobility, for state and pleasure.
Paris: III. 1.3. Feal-Chara.

The word *Feal-chara* means elephant's head: and the boat represented in the print take this name from their prow. They are become so scarce, that I met with but two or three of them during my stay in India, and these were used but in parties of pleasure. The Radjahs only, and rich people of the country, make use of them. Some old Hindoos, who had been in the service of great men, have assured me that they had formerly *Feal-charas* an hundred feet long by six. They have oars and sails. That which I have represented here was but fifty feet in length by four in breadth. This disproportion will be less striking when the reader becomes acquainted with what I shall say here after upon the naval construction of the Hindoos.

The *Feal-charas* are richly ornamented within and without; they move with a number of oars, one of which, of a larger size, is fixed in front, and in some sort steers this lengthly bark. The master or most distinguished personnage is seated before the rowers.

Commentary: The boat, as Solvyns states, takes its name from the elephant's head on the bow (prow)—in Hindustani, *fīl,* or Bengali, *pīl* (elephant) + *cehrā* (face), with the Hindustani form apparently in general use in Calcutta. The fīlcehrā, like the morpaṅkhī (Pl. 4), was one of a genre of long and narrow pleasure boats known generally as "snake boats," but the fīlcehrā must have been comparatively rare, belonging only to the exalted few.

In a letter of 1784, Warren Hastings wrote, "I intend to finish my voyage [to Calcutta] to-morrow in the feelchehra." Bustee footnotes Hasting's use of the word as "A large native boat; so called from the prow being commonly decorated with the figure of an elephant's head."[1]

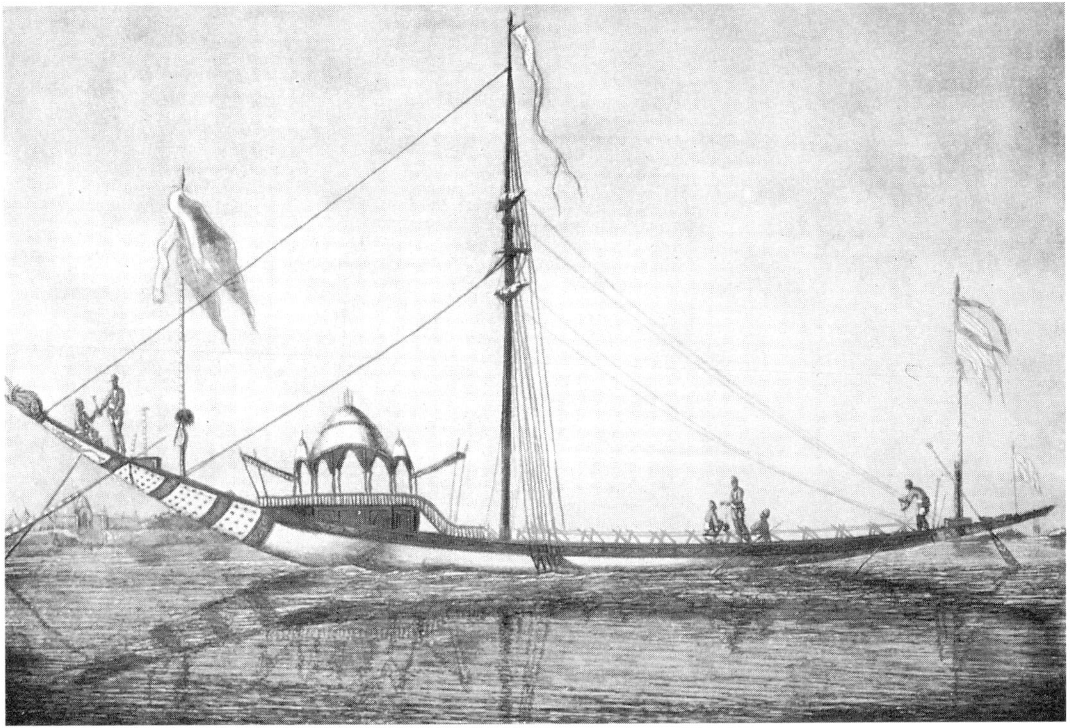

FĪLCHERĀ. Paris: III.1.3.

Bishop Heber, in an 1823 entry in his diary, described the "Feel Churra" belonging to the Governor of Bengal, Lord Amherst. The name, he relates, means "elephant bark, from having its head adorned with that of an elephant, with silver tusks. It is a large, light, and beautiful canoe, paddled by twenty men, who sit with their faces toward the head, with one leg hanging over the side of the boat, and the great toe through a ring fastened to its side. They keep time with their paddles, and join occasionally in chorus with a man who stands in the middle, singing.... In the fore-part of the boat is a small cabin, very richly ornamented, like the awnings in English barges, but enclosed with Venetian blinds; and between this and the head the mace-bearers of the Governor stand. The Union Jack is hoisted at the head and stern of the boat, and the Company's flag in the centre."[2] With sails and its slim elegance, it must have been an impressive boat.

NOTES

1 Hasting's letter in Busteed, 291. Hastings's fīlcehrā was later wrecked off Nayaserai. Suresh Chandra Ghosh, 140.

2 1:51-52. In his note to the drawing of the Morpaṅkhī (Pl. 4), Solvyns writes that the fīlcehrā, as the morpaṅkhī, is rowed to the song of a *jamadār* (leader).

4. Morpaṅkhī

Calcutta: Sec. VIII, No. 4. A Moorpunkee,—a Pleasure Boat used by the Natives.
Paris: III.1.4. Moor-punkee.

Moor-punkee means peacock's head. This boat is now in much more general use, and its construction is nearly the same as that of the *Feal-charra.* But the rowers use paddles, and are seated, with their faces to the prow. It is less expensive, though it is also richly ornamented. They are both very light and deserving of the attention of Europeans from the ingenuity of their construction. The prow and poop might be easily mistaken one for the other. The prince or leading person of the *Moor-punkee* is seated smoking his hooka under a particular canopy, in front of all the others. The grandees and servants of his retinue are under another awning. At the head of the rowers is a *Jemidar* [*jamadār*][1] who, by his voice and his motions, regulates the measure like the leader of an orchestra, and keeps the paddles to a regular movement. The comparison is apter from the little bells fastened to the paddles, which, shaken together, produce a sort of music. The *Magee* [*mājhī*] or pilot of the bark has a long oar with which he steers it.

Commentary: The morpaṅkhī (or mayūrpaṅkhī) takes its name from the boat's peacock bow and means, literally, "peacock feathered," but, as in Solvyns's account, it is sometimes described in English as "peacock's head."

In Solvyns's portrayal of the morpaṅkhī, there are some differences between the Calcutta and Paris etchings. In each, the hull of the boat is the same, but the canopy constructions are quite distinct. Also, in the Paris etching, the oarsmen wear red jackets; in the Calcutta etching, blue.

The morpaṅkhī and boats of similar character drew the attention of artist William Hodges, who noted their curious construction:

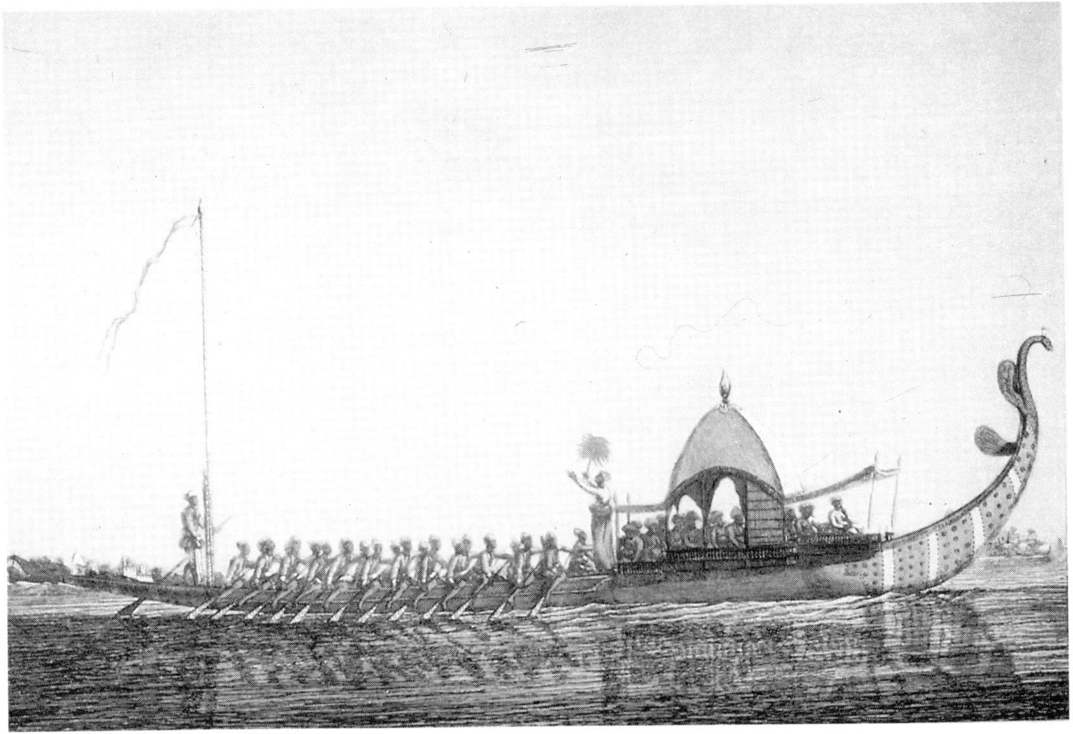

MORPAṄKHĪ. Paris: III.1.4.

"These [boats] are very long and narrow, sometimes extending upwards of an hundred feet in length, and not more than eight feet in breadth; they are always paddled, sometimes by forty men, and are steered by a large paddle from the stern, which rises either in the shape of a peacock, a snake, or some other animal. The persons employed to paddle are directed by a man who stands up, and sometimes he makes use of a branch or a plant to direct their motions. In one part of the stern is a canopy suppported by pillars, in which are seated the owner and his friends, who partake together of the refreshing breezes of the evening. These boats are very expensive, owing to the beautiful decorations of painted and gilt ornaments, which are highly varnished and exhibit a very considerable degree of taste."[2]

Solvyns provides a rich illustration for Hodge's account, with the standing *jamadār*—leader[3]—with a *chauṅrī* (wisk) in his hand, directing the oarsmen as if conducting an orchestra. And, indeed, these pleasure boats often took musicians for entertainment, one observer describing "the oars beating time to the notes of the clarionet."[4] In his note to the original drawing, Solvyns writes that the morpaṅkhī is paddled to the song of the *jamidār.*

In the note, Solvyns describes the morpaṅkhī as "A pleasure boat for princes and people of consequence in Hindostan." In Calcutta, the boats were especially popular for an evening's relaxation by European gentlemen and such wealthy Hindus as Kantababu, who owned one.[5]

One gentleman, the Marquess of Hastings, however, was not wholly enchanted. His diary for July 1814 carries the following entry: "A most splendit boat . . . a morpankha (peacock's feather) really elegant, but very inconvenient. The howdah or seat, near the bows, according to the fashion of those boats, was an extensive canopy of silver brocade divided into three domes, which were supported by silvered pillars. The body of the boat was painted with flowers on a yellow ground like a chintz. The effect was equally light and rich, but the howdah afforded little shelter from the sun. The boat must be from forescore to ninety feet long. Her head and stern were so high out of the water, that the man who managed the oar with which she was steered, easily communicated (by dancing) a springing motion to those who sat in the howdah."[6]

Both the morpaṅkhī and fīlcehrā were of a genre of pleasure boats termed "snake boats" for their length and quick daring motion.

These boats, described by a British officer in 1819, "are very narrow, and have large crews, who use short, broad paddles, with which they strike the water in a quick-measured cadence, which tells loudly, as it falls on the boat's gunwale. Here the owners are seated on cloths or carpets, with, or often without awnings; have their hookahs, and sherbet; a musician or two, or a story-teller: and the crews, too, sing accustomed airs with a wild chorus, led by their coxswain, who stands at the very stern, in a bold graceful attitude, as their boat darts on the bosom of the stream with fearful velocity."[7]

Lord Valentia, on his arrival in Bengal in 1803, described Governor Wellesley's "state barge"—apparently a snake boat—that transported him from his anchored ship upriver to Calcutta as something from a fairy tale: "It was very long in proportion to its width, richly ornamented with green and gold; its head, a spread eagle gilt; its stern, a tigers's head and body. The centre would contain twenty people with ease and was covered with an awning and side curtains: forward were seated twenty natives dressed in scarlet habits with rose-coloured turbans who paddled away with great velocity."[8]

Lady Nugent, in 1812, described perhaps the very same snake boat built by Wellesley. The boatmen, dressed in short pantaloons, scarlet jackets and turbans and sitting cross-legged, paddle in time with song or to the waving of "chowries" (*chauṅrī*)—"white cow's tails, set in silver handles"—by a man (very much as Solvyns depicts) standing in the center of the boat.[9]

By the time Yule and Burnell compiled *Hobson-Jobson* in 1886, these "state pleasure-boats on the Gangetic rivers" survived "only (if at all) at Murshīdābād."[10]

NOTES

1 *Jamadār* is the head of a group of men. See "Jemadar," in *Hobson-Jobson*, 458-59. (*Jamidār* is Bengali for *zamīndār*, landholder.)

2 *Travels in India*, 40. This description appears, without acknowledgement to Hodges, as a footnote by the translator of Stravorinus's *Voyages to the East Indies*, 1:467-68. The Rev. James Long quotes it, attributing it to Stavorinus in 1770 (see *Calcutta in the Olden Time*, 111), as does W.H. Carey, in 1882, perhaps simply borrowing from Long (see Wilson and Carey, *Glimpses*, 155). Raja Binaya Krishna Deb, 205, also follows Long.

3 In his note to the original drawing, Solvyns identifies the leader as a "*Sareewalla*," surely a mistake, for he correctly uses the term *jamidār* in the Paris text.

4 Quoted in Long, *Calcutta in the Olden Times,* 13.

5 Long, *Calcutta in the Olden Times,* 111. Nandy, 1:521. Nandy describes the boat as "peacock faced."

6 1:80-81.

7 *Sketches of India: Written by an Officer,* 166-67, quoted in Nair, *Calcutta in the 19th Century,* 219. Williamson, Pl. 12, *The European in India,* writes that fīlcherās and morpaṅkhis usually had from 30 to 50 oars and could proceed at 10 to 12 miles per hour, but could not compete with longer "snakes" that "absolutely dart through the water."

8 1:60, in Nair, *Calcutta in the 19th Century,* 2. In his note to the original drawing, Solvyns writes that the boat is paddled "to the song of a Sareewalla who with a chowry in his hand [who] displays the most ridiculous attitudes." Solvyns makes no such disparaging judgment in the 1799 *Catalogue* or in the Paris text, and his "Sareewalla" is probably a mistake for what should be *chauṅrīwala,* whisk-man.

9 78-80.

10 584.

5. Bājrā

Calcutta: Sec. VIII, No. 3. A Budgerow or Bengalee Barge.
Paris: III.1.5. Budgerow.

This, like the yatch [yacht] we have described [Pinnace, Pl. 2], is a boat hired for voyages on the rivers of Hindoostan: it is much higher in the poop and not so swift, so that it is eighteen of twenty days on a voyage which the other performs in fifteen. In other respects the *Budgerow* is extremely commodious, and with plenty of provisions, nothing is wanting in this sort of floating house. The kitchen and offices, as we have already mentioned, are in the attendant boats. We have but few such convenient barges in Europe, and travelling by water is in no part of the world so pleasant as in India. It is true that these voyages become very expensive from the quantity of things it is necessary to provide even for a few days: neither cloaths nor food must be forgotten, nor servants of every description, even washingmen and bakers. Each rower in Bengal has three roupees per month: the *Magee* [*mājhī*] or pilot the double; but they find themselves in cloaths and diet. The hire of a *Budgerow* may come to from three to five roupees a day. Among the *Magees* and *Dandys* [*dāṇḍī*] there are at present many Mussulmans who find employment even among the Hindoos, although the true followers of Brahma consider it as it duty to employ none but those of their own religion.

Commentary: Valued for its utility, the bājrā—Anglo-Indian budgerow or, less commonly, bazara[1] —was used by Europeans and prosperous Indians for traveling on the Ganges and its tributaries. Its early use by Europeans in Bengal is recorded by the seventeenth century traveler Thomas Bowrey: "A Budaroo Or Pleasure boat, wherein the English and Dutch Chiefe and Councill goe in State Upon the water, in Use alsoe by the Moors Grandees of Governours."[2]

Of all the boats of Bengal, the bājrā was most widely used by Europeans. In his "reminiscences of the good old days," William H.

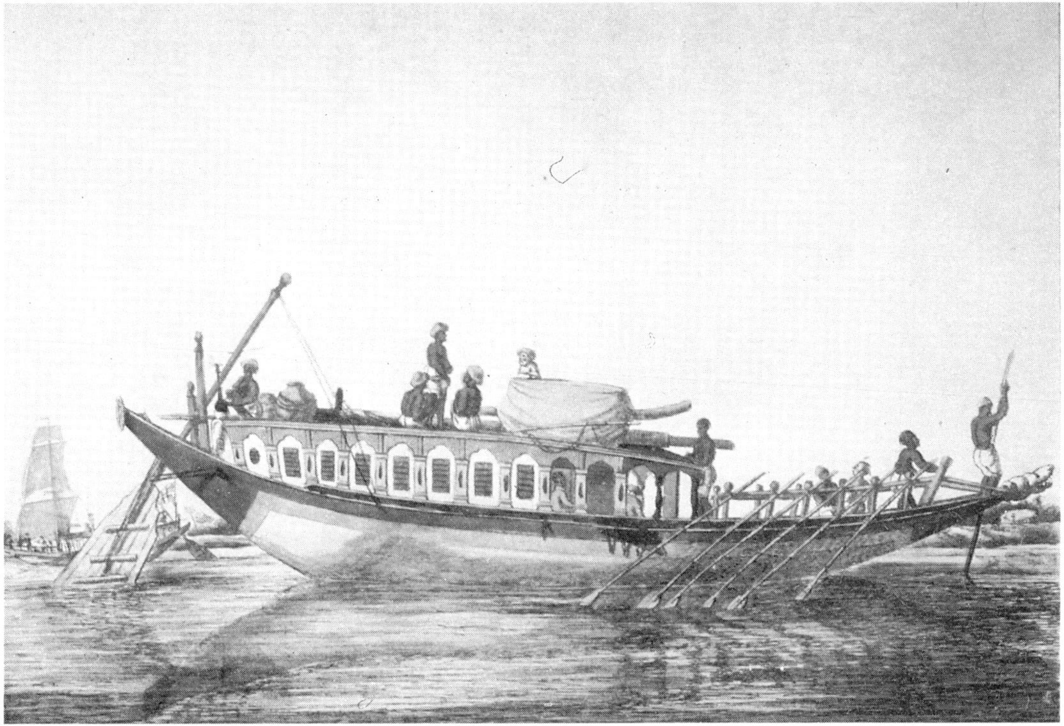

BĀJRĀ. Paris: III.1.5.

Carey, in 1882, wrote that "Budgerows are now extinct. Steamers nearly drove them off the river, and the railroad has extinguished them. But in days previous to steam navigation, they were the prinicipal conveyance for officers, and others proceeding to the north-western provinces."[3]

Flat-bottomed and drawing little water—a foot or a little more—the bājrā was sometimes described as a keelless barge. Bājrās were "large and commodious, but generally cumbrous and sluggish."[4] They varied in size, ranging from 25 to 60 feet or more in length, with a high stern that rose as much as 12 feet above the water. The stern apparently varied from the sharp point seen in Solvyns's etching to spoon or sometimes square shapes, and the prow might be ornamented with a figurehead such as that described by Carey: "a hideous attempt at an European, with a black hat, a bright blue coat, and a yellow waistcoat."[5] In Solvyns's portrayal, the bow is fitted with the head of what appears to be a crocodile with gaping mouth.

The bājrā, though less luxurious than the pinnace, provided considerable comfort. Some two-thirds of the aft portion were given to cabins, with venetianed windows that could be lifted along each side. A verandah in front opened at the same level into the sitting and dining room, with a ceiling height of some seven to nine feet. Toward the stern and rising one or two steps were either one or two sleeping cabins, each usually with a small toilet closet, or head. Toward the fore, the bājrā was decked and equipped with two covered hatchways.[6] The roof was flat and was used by passengers as a promenade deck in the evening and as a place for the crew and servants to sleep at night.

With a crew under the *mājhī*, bājrās typically had ten to twenty oars. In Solvyns's portrayal, the bājrā is manned by twelve oarsmen, *dāṇḍīs*. The oars are long poles with a small oval board afixed at the end. Stavorinus, from his travels, 1768-1771, notes that "they do not strike the water cross ways, but obliquely backwards."[7] The *mājhī*, at the helm on the upper deck, steered the boat by a large rudder extending from the stern. With the danger of the boat's running aground, a "*goleer*" (also *golea, golia*) at the bow determines the depth of the water by means of a long oar or bamboo pole.[8]

Although Solvyns's bājrā is not shown with the mast raised, to take advantage of any winds, bājrās were equipped with a single square-rigged mast. Hornell describes the mast as fixed and stepped amidships, with a slender topmast usually added. "The mainsail is square with a bamboo yard along the upper margin; in fine weather a square topsail is hoisted above the mainsail."[9] With a crosswind, the boat, without a keel, would move forward transversely.[10]

As flat-bottomed boats, bājrās did not sail well and were dangerous in the wind and, top-heavy, could be easily overturned.[11] But the artist William Hodges writes in 1781 that "the English gentlemen have made great improvements on the budgerow in Bengal, by introducing a broad flat floor, square sterns, and broad bows. These boats are much safer, sail near and keep their wind, and there is no danger attending their taking the ground; they are besides, calculated for carrying a greater quantity of sail."[12]

But the bājrā's progress upriver was usually by neither sail nor oar. Rather it was towed, "tracked," along the edge of the shore by a line some 80 to 100 yards long, with the crew laboring in relays throughout the day.[13]

Mrs. Kindersley, in a letter from Patna in 1766, described her bājrā journey:

> The progress up the Ganges is so exceedingly slow, that the voyage from Calcutta to Allahabad takes nearly three months to perform it in; at the same time that it is common to go from Allahabad to Calcutta in twenty days. . . .
>
> [I]n the passage up the river they most tow; but when they [*dāṇḍīs*] come to a creek, of which there are many very broad, they fasten the rope round their wastes, and, throwing themselves from the land, which is often very high, swim across, dragging the *budgeroo* after them.
>
> When the squalls of wind and rain come on, if they can find no place to lay by, they jump into the river, and hang with their hands upon the edge of the boat, to keep it steady, with just their mouth above the water. . . The work of towing, or as it is called, tracking, is sometimes exceedingly laborious; for the banks, which, when the river is lowered, are the height of a house at least above the water, are so softened by the rains, that *dandies* sink midleg at every step they take; frequently large pieces of the banks give way, and by their fall boats are sunk or overset.
>
> Sometimes they row; then it is they seem to enjoy themselves, singing all together, with great vehemence, some songs peculiar to their employment.
>
> A family has frequently two *budgeroos*, besides boats; one of the boats is for cookery, the others for servants, provisions, furniture, and other necessities; for whenever people remove from one place to another, they are obliged to carry all these things with them, even *palenqueens*, carriages, and horses; so that the troop of attendants of every kind amounts to a great number of people.
>
> When once chooses to dine, &c. the *budgeroo* is stopped, and the boats which are wanted come round it, and dinner is served with as much order as on shore. . . .

Except in the squalls, which are frequent in the season, it is a most easy method of traveling, and, when a party of *budgeroos* go together, very agreeable.

When the *budgeroos* stop at night, the *dandies* make their fires on shore, each *cast* by themselves. . . .[14]

In the eighteenth and early nineteenth century, European travelers in Bengal frequently describe their river trips by *bājrā* and, like Mrs. Kindersley, refer to *dandies* at the oars. Captain G.C. Mundy notes that "The crews are of either sect, Mussulman or Hindoo; the former are, perhaps, the more able-bodied seamen, and stauncher at the oar. . . . The dandies," he writes, "are generally fine, stout and sleek figures. In rowing they stand upright, advancing and retiring two or three steps at every stroke; and lightening their labour, as well as preserving the measure, by a song and chorus."[15]

With one or two bājrās and their attendant boats, the river convoy included, at a minimum, a pulwār (Pl. 29) as a kitchen boat and a smaller, more manouverable pānsi (Pl. 9), used to convey bājrā passengers to shore and back.[16] For longer trips and those with heavy or substantial freight, one or more separate baggage boats accompanied the bājrā, providing both storage for goods and chattel and accommodation for an overflow of servants.

The stock for a long voyage upriver would consist of "groceries of all kinds, wine, beer, and brandy, salt provisions, tongues, hams, tamarind-fish (fish cured with the acid of the tamarind), flour, biscuits, and charcoal; a dozen or two of live fowl and ducks, and a couple of milch goats."[17]

Atop the bājrā, in Solvyns's portrayal, is a long palanquin, covered by a tarpaulin and awaiting use on land by the European party.

NOTES

1 *Hobson-Jobson*, 120.

2 228.

3 "Sidelights and Reminiscences of the Good Old Days," 1882, in Wilson and Carey, 184.

4 Colesworthy Grant, *Rural Life in Bengal*, 5, with a small engraving.

5 "Sidelights and Reminiscencs of the Good Old Days," 1882, in Wilson and Carey, 184.

6 Williamson, *East India Vide-Mecan*, 377.

7 465-66.

8 "Sketches of Indian Society: No. VI, Travelling—the Buderow," *Asiatic Journal*, 12 (September-December 1833), 13-14, quoted in Nair, *British Social Life*, 60-61. Solvyns's "goleer" for bowman is probably from the Bengali *golui*, bow. On the perils of running aground, see Bernstein, 18-19.

9 *Water Transport*, 246. Also see Hornell, "The Boats of the Ganges," 185-87.

10 Stavorinus, 465-66; Hodges, *Travels*, 39; and Grant and Colebrooke, 115.

11 Bacon, quoted in Nair, *Calcutta in the 19th Century*, 561-62.

12 *Travels*, 40.

13 Carey, "Sidelights and Reminiscences of the Good Old Days," 1882, in Wilson and Carey, 185.

14 Kindersley, 93-97; reprinted in Nair, *Calcutta in the 18th Century*, 141-42. Kindersley provides one of the earliest accounts of travel by bājrā, but descriptions of the bājrā are frequent in subsequent accounts of European life in Bengal. See, for example, Nugent, 2:371-72; *Sketches of India*, in Nair, *Calcutta in the 19th Century*, 192-93; Fenton, 29-30, in Nair, *Calcutta in the 19th Century*, 457-58; Mundy, 2:147-51, in Nair, *Calcutta in the 19th Century, 485-86;* Roberts, 2nd ed., 1:261-93; and Dewar, *In the Days of the Company*, 64-74. Thomas Williamson and Gilchrist, 450-471, in manuals for Europeans coming to India for the first time, provide detailed instructions for outfitting these bājrā flotillas.

15 1:149-50; reprinted in Nair, *Calcutta in the 19th Century*, 486.

16 Hodges, *Travels*, 39.

17 "Sketches of Indian Society: No. VI, Travelling—the Budgerow," *Asiatic Journal*, 12 (September-December 1833), 13-14, quoted in Nair, *British Social Life*, 60-61.

6. Bhāuliyā

Calcutta: Sec. VIII, No. 5. A Baawalee-a, a large narrow Boat for expedition.
Paris: III.1.6. Baawalee-a.

This species of boat is the swiftest we know. The extreme lightness of its construction gives it incredible speed. An example among others is cited of a governor general, who in his *Baawalee-a* performed in eight days the voyage from Lucknow to Calcutta, a distance of four hundred marine leagues. This fact is attested by several persons: it is true the governor took care to have frequent changes of rowers at proper distances.

Though the number of rowers seem to increase the speed, experience has proved that too many impede it. The middle-sized *Baawalee-as* have but six or eight, and they are the best: they go against wind and tide. They differ from the *Moor-punkee* [Pl. 4] by the height of the poop above the prow, and by not having so many conveniences. The master is seated behind the rowers, near the Magee [*mājhī*]. No one can change his place without giving a shock to the whole boat; it is so light and so narrow.

Commentary: The bhāuliyā (bhāule in modern Bengali)[1] is a long, narrow Bengali river boat with generally four to eight oars. Hornell contrasts the smaller and more manageable bhāuliyā with the leisurely, if sometimes cumbersome bājrā: "with a lusty crew rowing cheerfully to a rhythmic chant it carries its passengers swiftly along, even against the stream."[2] Most descriptions give it one small cabin, but Solvyns depicts what *Hobson-Jobson* refers to as "only a small kiosque at the stern."[3] Grant, in *Rural Life in Bengal*, includes an illustration of the bhāuliyā with not only a cabin but a mast.[4] The mast in the better bhāuliyās is hinged in a tabernacle; others rely simply on a pole that is taken aboard as needed.[5]

Buchanan, in the early 1800s, writes that the bhāuliyā, like the pānsi (Pl. 9), is a passenger boat. "It is sharp at both ends, rises at the

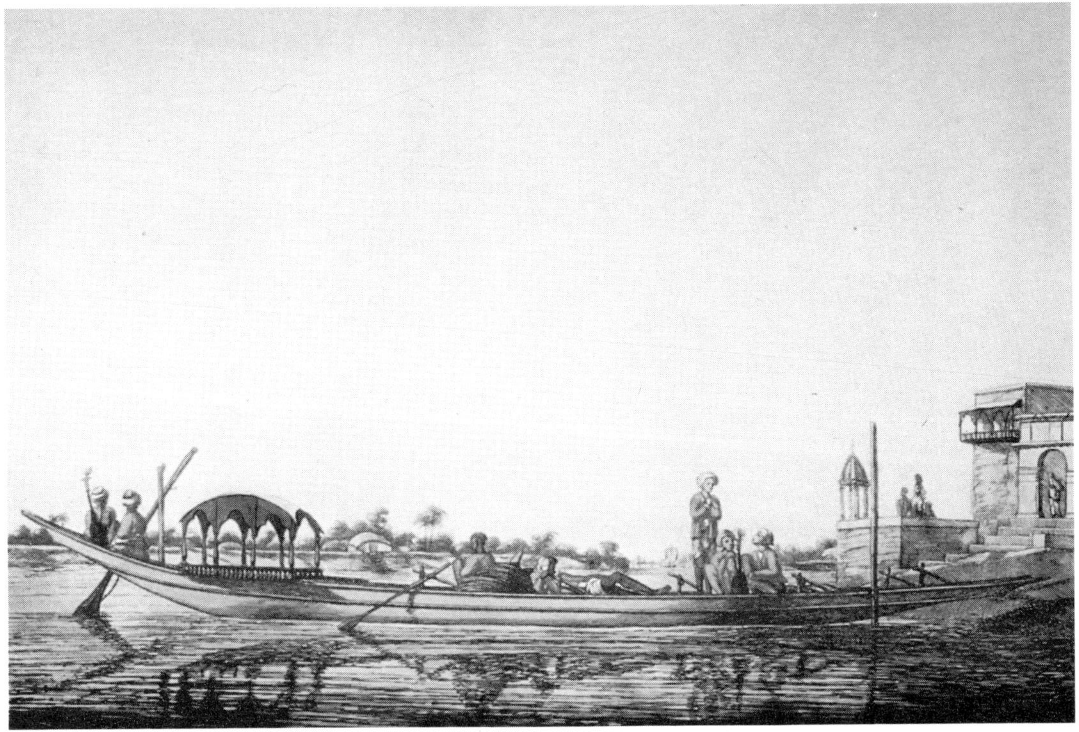

BHĀULIYĀ. Paris: III.1.6.

ends less than the *Pansi,* and its tilt is placed in the middle, the rowers standing both before and behind the place of accommodation of passengers." But reflecting the variation of names for boats in eastern India, Buchanan notes, "On the Kosi [river in northeastern Bihar], the *Bhauliya* is a large fishing-boat, carrying six or seven men."[6]

NOTES

1 Sukumar Sen, 704; *Hobson-Jobson,* "boliah," 102.
2 Hornell, "The Boats of the Ganges," 187.
3 102.
4 3.
5 Hornell, "The Boats of the Ganges," 188.
6 As related in Montgomery Martin, 3:345.

7. Bore

Calcutta: Before Sec. VIII. A View of the coming in of the Bhaun [ban] or Boar, in Garden Reach.
Paris: III.2.1. The Coming in of the Bhaun or Boar.

This number begins, like the preceding one, with the representation of a phenomenon of nature, the *Macree,* or tide at the mouth of the river Ougly [Hugli]. It is well known that the tide in general is strongest where it meets with least resistance. In the Indian seas its force is uncontrouled by any obstacle; which is probably the cause of its extraordinary violence in the Ougly: in less than five minutes, it rises to the height of fifteen to twenty feet and is impelled with such impetuosity that it carries off immense banks of sand, and forces the river out of its natural bounds, and as it were from its very foundations. Woe to the vessels which have not had the prudence to quit it at this time: the tide is most violent where the water is less deep: the waves at times glide along the sides, raise up the sand-banks, and dash through the river to the other side where the current is strongest. The noise is dreadful and heard at a great distance, especially in the night. I have endeavoured to give a representation of all the terrible scenes which the *Macree* produces, but I must confess that they are much more faithfully preserved in the imagination than by the graver. The view is in the environs of Calcutta; the horizon is bounded by magnificent private gardens, the botanical garden, etc.

The *Macree* is most to be feared in the months of march and april, particularly with a southerly wind: it is also very violent in the quadratures and oppositions of the moon.

Commentary: A bore—*bān* in Bengali—is "a sudden and abrupt influx of the tide into a river or narrow strait."[1] Solvyns uses *macrée* as French for bore. The word, according to *Hobson-Jobson,* is associated with *macareo,* "a term applied by old voyagers to the phenomenon of the *bore* . . . [and] used by them as if it were an Oriental word."[2]

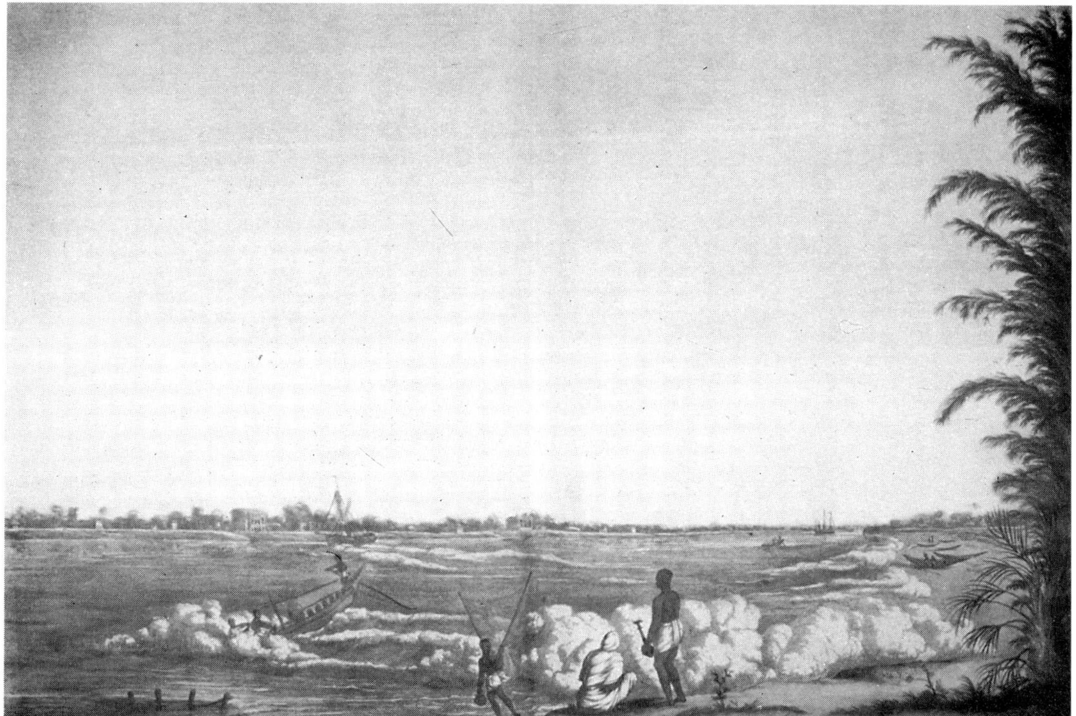

BORE. Paris: III.2.1. (double plate)

Milbourn, in *Oriental Commerce,* describes the bore on the Hugli: "So quick is its motion, that it hardly employs four hours in traveling" some 70 miles upriver. "At Calcutta, it sometimes occasions an instantaneous rise of five feet; and both here and in every part of its track, the boats on its approach immediately quite the shore, and make for safety to the middle of the river."[3] This spring tidal rush passes rapidly and involves a "tremendous noise"—a sound, Bishop Heber wrote, that resembled a steam-boat, but "infinitely louder."[4]

In Solvyns's etching, a pānsi (Pl. 9) struggles against the bore, as a Jāliyā, fisherman,[5] with his nets, walks along the river bank.

William Daniell portrayed *The Bore Rushing Up the Hoogley* in a dramatic engraving for the *Oriental Annual* of 1837.[6]

NOTES

1 Milbourn, 251.

2 527.

3 251. Also see Williamson, *East-India Vide-Mecam,* 2:231-37.

4 1:74.

5 Solvyns portrays in the Jāliyā in an etching, Calcutta: Sec. I. No. 57, and Paris: I.9.6.

6 Engraving by R. Brandard, after the drawing by Daniell. Opp. 224.

8. Paṭuā

Calcutta: Sec. IX, No. 5. A Pettooa,—a Balasore Boat.
Paris: III.2.2. Pettoo-a.

This is the name given to some boats which come from Balassora or the coast of Palmira [in Orissa]. The *Pettoo-as* differ from other vessels by their being clincherbuilt [clinker-built]: the boards are one upon the other, contrary to our European construction of that kind: they are fastened by little pieces of iron in the form of cramps. The anchors are often of wood, but they are not at present much in use. The yard is always without sail, and the sails are hoisted and lowered by blocks. The *Pettoo-as* are very crank, and cannot keep close to the wind: for which reason they always wait for the fine monsoon to sail: they seldom go alone. On their return upon their ballast they appear always on the point of turning over, from their excessive lightness: the weight of a single man on either side is sufficient to make them dip several feet. They are generally manned with *Ourihas* [Oriyas]: when they arrive, they run them a-shore on the sand, and haul them up dry with the paras[1] so much used in the Mediterranean, waiting prudently for the fine weather to return. The *Pettoo-as* are provided with large *jars* to hold their water. The cordage called *cariar* [coir], is generally made of the filaments of the cocoa-nut. The engraving will give a sufficient idea of the form of the *Pettoo-a.*

Commentary: The paṭuā is a sea-going boat of Orissa, but rather unstable ("crank") and liable to capsize in rough water. Solvyns describes its hull in terms that suggest reverse clinker construction. In this ancient form, depicted in two carvings of boats from eleventh-twelfth century Orissa, "the overlaps are reversed, that is, the upper edge of the lower plank is outside the lower edge of the upper plank."[2]

In the etching, following convention, the boats in the distance are likely paṭuās at sail.

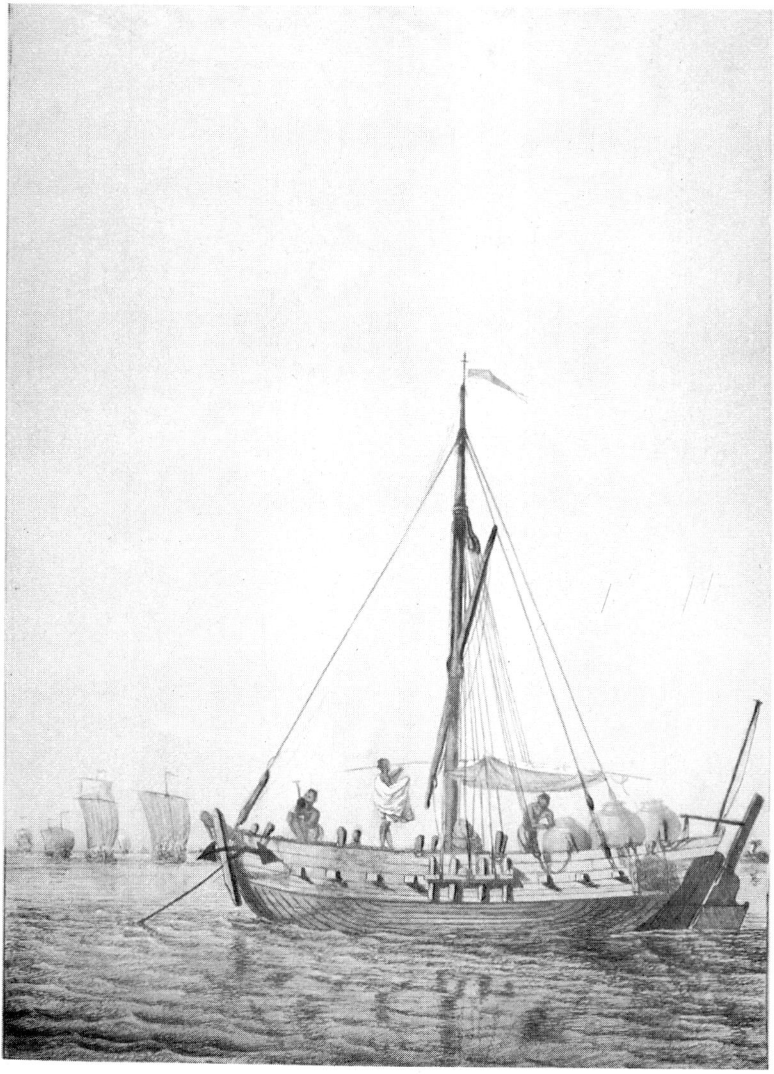

PAṬUĀ. Paris: III.2.2.

NOTES

1 The French word *para* refers to a construction to hoist a boat onto land. Fennis, 3:1346.

2 Deloche, 2:170.

9. Pānsi

Calcutta: Sec. VIII, No. 6. A Punsway, a small convenient passage Boat.
Paris: III.2.3. Pansway.

The *Pansway* is a passage-boat very convenient for inland navigation. At Calcutta *Pansways* of different sizes are to be met with in all the *gauts* or wharfs, which convey passengers to the towns upon the rivers: in general they have but four oars and a *Magie* [*mājhī*] or pilot, and are hired for about a *roupee* or half-crown a day.

The *Pansways* are convenient only for a short passage: the seat under the awning is not easy; there is no kitchen: so that the dinner must be prepared on shore.

There are others which carry six oars, and are better equipped: those go down the river to take passengers to and from the ships. Others of a still larger size are used to carry rice and provisions to a great distance up the rivers. These are generally manned by Hindoos, as the others are by Mussulmans and men of all casts. The *Pansways* appropriated to passengers are painted with a bad sort of colours. There are some also of this kind which carry sail pretty well: but they cannot go close to the wind.

Commentary: The pānsi (Anglo-Indian, paunchway or, less commonly, pansway) is a light river boat of Bengal, rather like a large ḍiṅgi (Pl.11). It is typically 20 to 30 feet in length, with a roof of matting or thatch, a mast that may be stepped in front, and with three to six oars.[1] Grant and Colebrooke suggest that the name "seems to import that it should carry 500 muns [maunds], but in practice this boat varies much in size; it is of light draught, and outstrips a Pinnace before the wind."[2]

According to *Admiral Paris' Native Boats,* "There are a great variety in the line and size of this name; they have no keel, are longer and less flat than 'dinghis', and are easier to sail. They have a framework, and their planking is joined by cramp-irons, and pierced by the

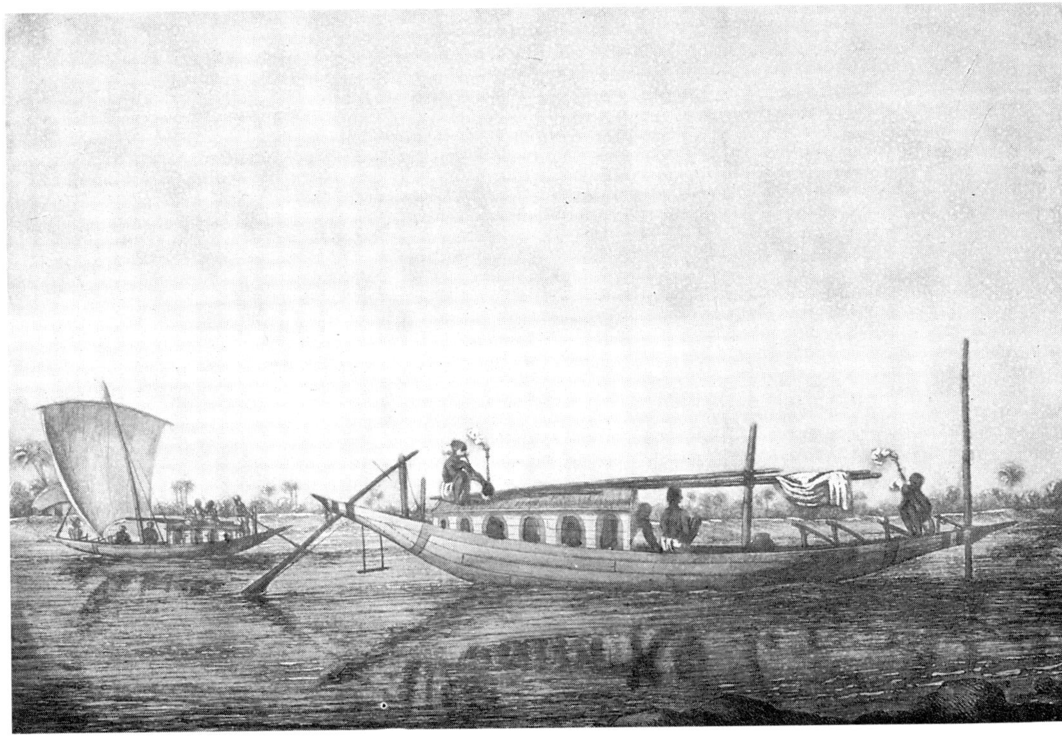

PĀNSI. Paris: III.2.3.

beams. Almost all carry a cabin made of planks and matting, with a thatched roof. 'Pansways' carry an upper platform towards the rear only, and only if their rudder is vertical (usually they use an oar attached to a structure of posts.)."[3]

The pānsi, described by Kerchove, is "a double-ended open boat with long overhangs covered at the after-end with a bamboo and mat thatch. It is employed for transportation of goods and passengers on the Estuary of the Ganges River, Bengal. Iron wood is used for the bottom planking, teak for the sides and sal wood for the upper works and beams."[4]

As related in various accounts of the bājrā (Pl. 5), a pānsi typically accompanied the larger boat to convey passengers back and forth to shore. The pānsi has the same general construction as the bājrā, with the difference, artist William Hodges relates, "that the greatest breadth is somewhat further aft, and the stern lower."[5]

It was by pānsi that William Hickey arrived in Calcutta from anchorage at Sagar Island, some 100 miles down river at the mouth of the Hugli. "This mode of traveling did not exactly meet our approbation, paunceways being so constructed that you have not room to sit upright under the roof or covering of mat to protect those within from sun or rain, nor is there any place to let your legs hang down in, passengers sitting upon a platform like tailors on their shopboard."[6]

Bishop Heber, in 1823, also arrived in Calcutta from Sagar by pānsi. In his diary, he recorded that

> a "Panchway," or passsage boat, . . . was a very characteristic and interesting vessel, large and broad, shaped like a snuffer dish; a deck fore and aft, and the middle covered with a roof of palm branches, over which again was lashed a coarse cloth, the whole forming an excellent shade from the sun; but, as I should apprehend, intolerably close. The "serang," or master, stood on the little after-deck, steering with a long oar; another man, a little before him, had a similar oar on the starboard quarter; six rowers were seated cross-legged on the deck upon the tilt, and plied their short paddles with much dexterity; not however as paddles usually are plied, but in the manner of oars, resting them instead of rullocks, on bamboos, which rose upright from the sides. A large long sail of thin transparent sackcloth in three pieces, very loosely tacked to each other, completed the equipment.[7]

The etching provides a good illustration of the convention in marine painting of varied views of the boat, with the pānsi in the background with mast stepped and sails unfurled.

NOTES

1 *Hobson-Jobson,* 688; Deloche, 2:162; and Hornell, "The Boats of the Ganges," 181.
2 116.
3 37-39.
4 517.
5 40; also see Stavorinus, 1:467fn.
6 Hickey, 2:117-118.
7 1:5-6. An engraving illustrates a "Calcutta Panchway."

10. Khelā or Lāl Ḍiṅgi

Calcutta: Sec. VIII, No. 9. A Khela or Loll Dingee,—the common pleasure Boat of the Natives, and used by Europeans for expedition.
Paris. III.2.4. Khela or Loll Dingee.

These are boats of a very slight construction, generally used by persons who live near the river. The *Circars* come to town for their business in a *Khelā* on which they bestow more or less ornament. The *Khelā-Dingee* represented in the engraving is of the plainer sort: it is worked by two rowers: the master is stretched out indolently, while his companions are smoking the hooka.

The Hindoo oar consists of a cross-grained board tied to a bambou: to put it in motion they use another smaller bambou fastened to the first with a hempen cord.

The rowers of these little boats are far from being as dexterous as the other Hindoo workmen; there is always something wanting in their tackle: and when any accident happens, they are quite at a loss, and are satisfied with calling God to their assistance, without endeavouring to help themselves.

Commentary: The boat is a variety of *ḍiṅgi*, the word *khelā* meaning pleasure or sport. "Loll" carries no suggestion of nautical meaning, but it is likely *lāl*, "red," as one might well imagine Solvyns asking the boatman, "What do you call this boat?" and the man replies, "*lāl ḍiṅgi*, sahib." Solvyns, however, does not portray a "red" boat. In the Calcutta etching, the fore rail is blue and there is a red gunwale; in the Paris etching, these colors are reversed.

The boat in the background is a *khelā ḍiṅgi* with sail.

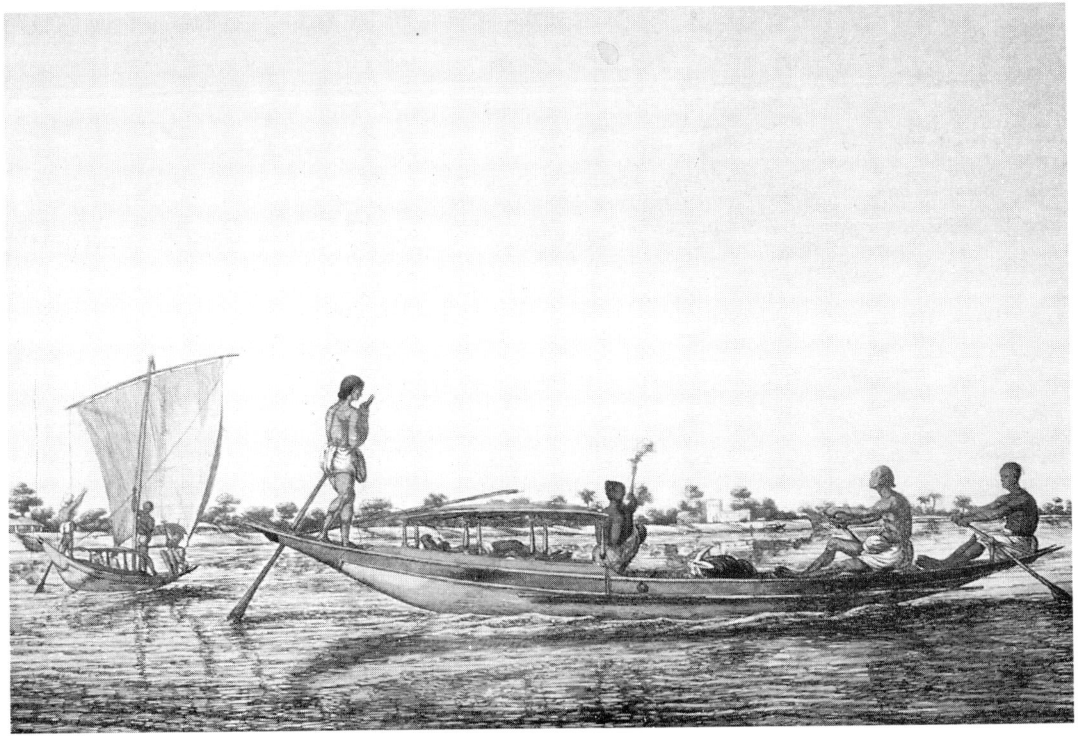

KHELĀ OR LĀL ḌIṄGI. Paris: III.2.4.

11. Ḍiṅgi

Calcutta: Sec. VIII, No. 8. A Dingee,—a general name for every small boat. Paris: III.2.5. Dingee.

Although the word *Dingee* means a boat in general, it is more particularly applied to a sort of boat used to keep up the communication between the ships and the different ports and landing-places. Vast numbers of these *Dingees* ply all along the port of Calcutta, and for a meer trifle you may be carried aboard the ships. While a vessel is at anchor before the town, the *Dingees* perform a regular service in carrying provisions, and supplying the crews with whatever they may want. In this case they are hired by the month.

Some *Dingees* have one or even two rowers, but in general they are managed by a single man with one oar in the poop. This will not appear extraordinary to those who know that in some countries, as in China for example, vessels of some hundred tons are worked by the motion of a single oar in the stern.

Commentary: Ḍiṅgi, in Bengali, means "small boat"—the diminutive of *ḍiṅgā*, "boat"[1]—and, with a variety of shapes and sizes, it resembles a canoe or wherry.[2] The word entered English as "dinghy" to refer to a small boat carried as a tender, lifeboat, or pleasure craft on a larger boat, and also to a small rowboat.[3] With a brig in the background of the etching, Solvyns suggests such an use here.

In North India, the term is used to mean a dugout, hollowed from a tree trunk, but in Bengal, the word generally refers to half-decked, round-bottomed boats build of planks, fastend with nails or boatbuilders stables, or, as perhaps here in Solvyns's portrayal, sewn together. Manned usually by two rowers toward the front and a steersman at the stern, the *ḍiṅgi* is "of slight construction, spoon-bottomed, with a circular awning of bamboo-work, under which a person can sit. . . ."[4]

Ḍiṅgis were used for river passage of short duration, as in ferry-crossings from Calcutta to the opposite shore, for fishing, and in transport back and forth from ship to shore, as Solvyns here portrays.

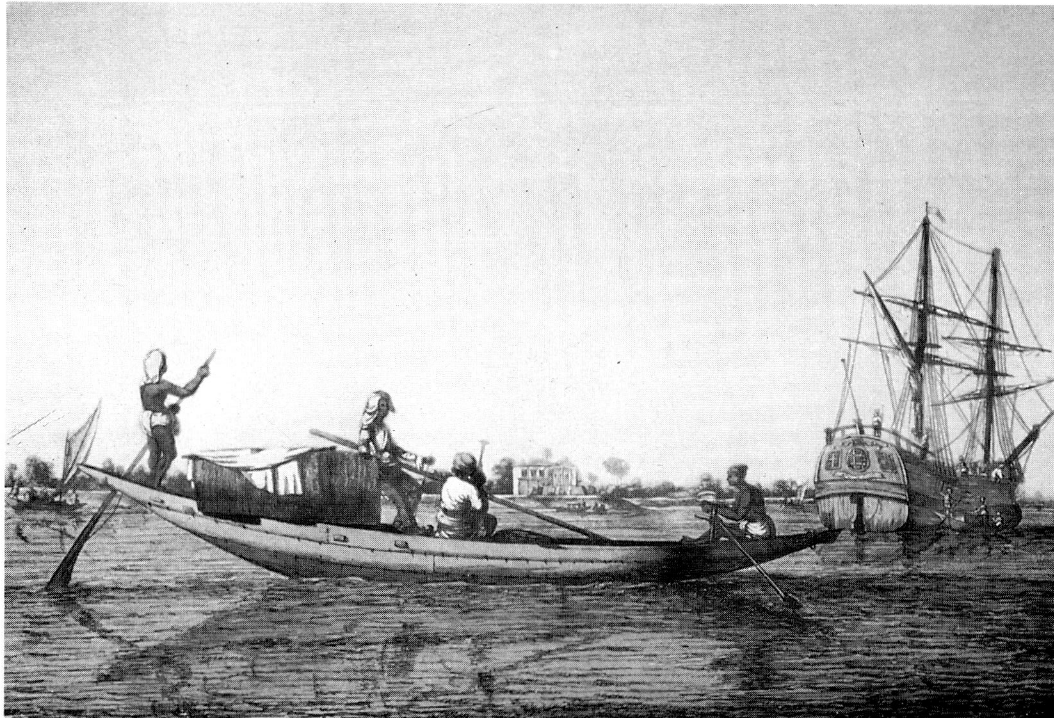

ḌIṄGI. Paris: III.2.5.

NOTES

1 Sukumar Sen, 375.
2 Hornell, *Water Transport,* illustrates four types of ḍiṅgis, 242-44.
3 *American Heritage Dictionary.* Also see *Hobson-Jobson,* 318.
4 Stocqueler, *Hand-Book of British India,* 185. Also see Grant and Colebrooke, 115; and Deloche, 2:158.

12. Magarcehrā

Calcutta: Sec. VIII, No. 12. A Muga Chara,—a Dacca Boat, commonly hired by the lower class to celebrate their marriages, festivals and parties of pleasure. Paris: III.2.6. Muga-Chara.

This species of boat is seldom seen at Calcutta, but is much used in upper Hindoostan, especially in Dacca. In this country, which is traversed by rivers and canals, passengers are conveyed by the *Muga-charas,* and sometimes in great multitudes, as at feasts and marriages. I have here given the representation of a wedding travelling in one of these boats. The palanqueen, the musicians, and all that characterises this solemnity, are seen in the engraving. On such occasions several boats are necessary; and it is not uncommon therefore to see *Muga-charas* accompanied by *Pulwars, Pansways,* and other vessels. The fore-part or prow of the *Muga-chara* is higher than the poop, and is ornamented with a head and other figures, like the *Feal-chara* and *Moor-Punkee.* It is covered with double or triple mats, which, though extremely light, are a sufficient protection against the rain.

Commentary: As with the fīlcehrā, the name refers to the "face" on the bow of the boat. Here, Solvyns's "muga" (Anglo-Indian, muggur or muggar) is *magar,* the broad-snouted marsh crocodile of the Ganges.[1] Solvyns's portrays what at first glance appears more like an elephant with a curving trunk, but the sharp teeth reveal what is a rather peculiar crocodile. No reference to a boat of this name appears in the literature consulted.

The boat is fitted with a *chāunri,* a thatched shelter, typically (as here) of woven bamboo that is bent over to make a tunnel-like covering for crew and passengers.[2]

The wedding party, to which Solvyns refers, is shown in a magarcehrā along the shore. A palanquin, for the bride, is aboard, as are musicians with a rāmśiṅgā[3] and bā̃k,[4] more clearly evident in the Paris than the Calcutta etching.

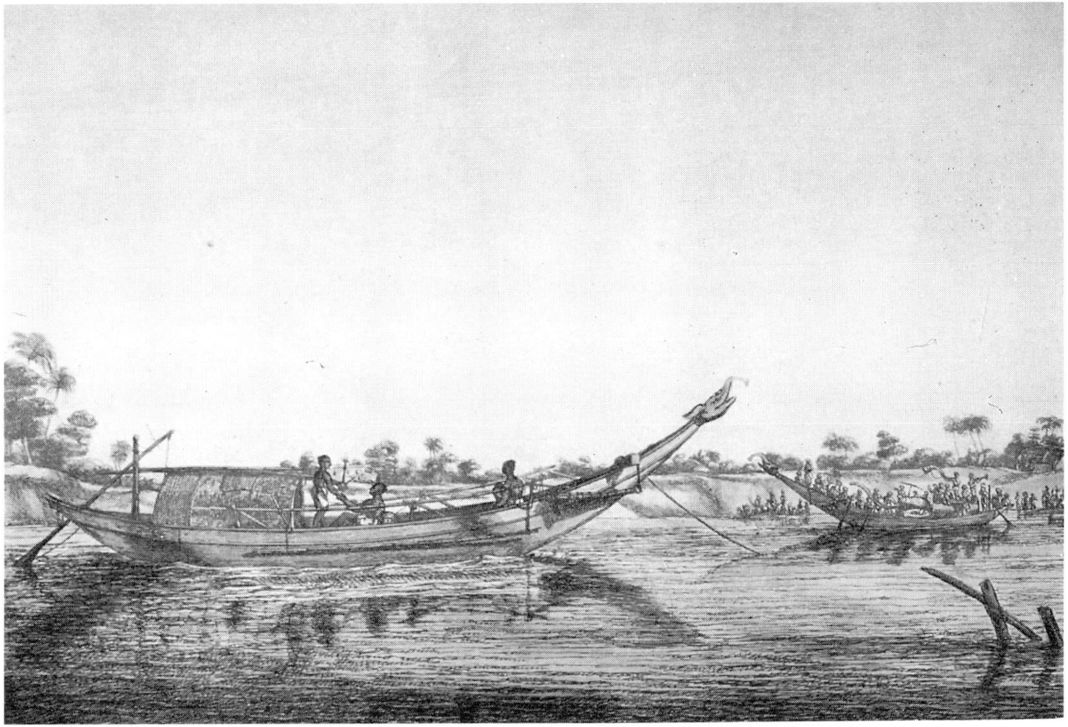

MAGARCEHRĀ. Paris: III.2.6.

NOTES

1 *Hobson-Jobson*, 595. For a description of the magar (*Crocodylus palustris*), see Daniel, 10-12.

2 Greenhill, *Boats and Boatmen of Pakistan*, 28.

3 Portrayed by Solvyns, Calcutta: Sec. XI, No. 30; Paris: II.12.2, and included in Hardgrave and Slawek, 129-31.

4 Portrayed by Solvyns, Calcutta: Sec. XI, No. 23; Paris, II.12.3, and included in Hardgrave and Slawek, 132-34.

13. Penang

Paris: III.3.1. Poulo Penang.

The island of *Penang,* now called prince of Wales's, island, is situated to the north of the straits of Malacca; this view of it is taken on the side of the fort. It is one of the most beautiful and fertile islands on the Indian coast, and belongs to England, under the administration of a governor. Fish, fruits and grain are found here in the greatest abundance; the mangastan [mangosteen] especially (the *garcinia* of Linneus) is delicious.

The inhabitants are mostly of Malayan origin; there are also a number of Chinese, who have their temples, their playhouses, and a great many gaming houses, on which the governor levies a considerable tax: these houses, which are always open on the side of the street, are much frequented, and particularly by the class of workmen who often quit their work to game.

There are in the island several distilleries of arrak belonging to the Chinese, which pay also considerable duties to the governor, and are deserving of the attention of Europeans.

The island of *Penang* is frequented by a great number of boats of different sizes from the neighbouring islands, whose productions they bring to its magnificent bazar. One species of these vessels, the *proues,* is used by the Malays in their piratical expeditions in the straits but more to the south of Malacca these pirates are frequently in great force, and are not intidated by strong armed ships: they take advantage of the night or of a calm to endeavour to board them; they use poisoned *crests* [*krīs*].[1] And massacre the crews. These boats, of which several are represented in the engraving are excellent sailors, light and well manned, they carry square sails, and some of them one, two, or three masts; their construction is neat and light.

Commentary: The print does not appear in the Calcutta edition, and it is likely that Solvyns visited Penang only in 1803, on his return voyage to Europe. The route from Calcutta typically crossed the Bay

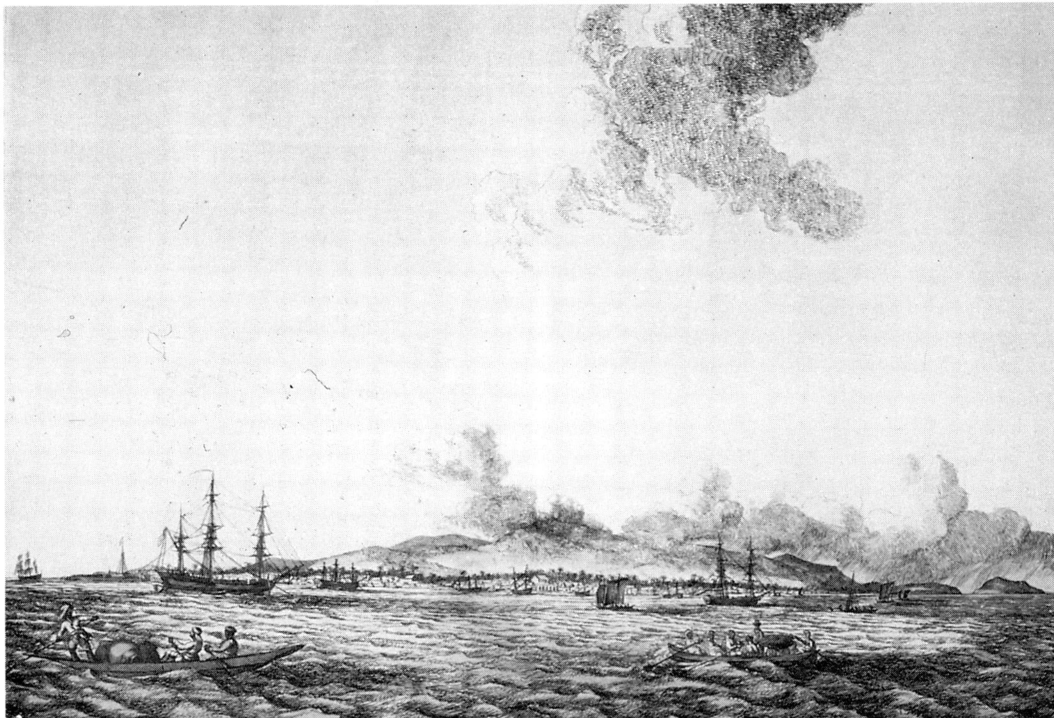

PENANG. Paris: III.3.1. (double plate)

of Bengal to stop at Penang and from there to Madras and on around the tip of India.

Solvyns's *Poulo* is the Malay *pulau*, "island," and *piŋang* is the word for areca-nut or -tree.[2] The British took possession of the island in 1786, naming it "Prince of Wales Island," but this in turn gave way to the Malay name.

Solvyns's "proue" is the Malay *praū*, or *prahū* (proa in English; *prao* in Portuguese), a particular kind of galley used in the Straits and the archipelago, but the term is used generally for any Malay native craft, though usually small craft.[3]

NOTES

1 A Malay dagger: "creese" in the *Oxford English Dictionary*; "crease" in *Hobson-Jobson*, 274, from the Malay *krīs*.

2 *Hobson-Jobson*, 695, and Walter Hamilton, *East India Gazetteer*, 2:418.

3 *Hobson-Jobson*, 733, and Noel.

14. Donī

Calcutta: Sec. IX, No. 4. A Dony,—a clumsy Craft, from the Coromandel Coast.
Paris: III.3.2. Dony.

This is the name of a very unwieldy boat with one mast, resembling a sloop: its deck consists of a few planks fastened on each side: it is badly rigged, and sails but in the favorable monsoon. It comes from the coast of Coromandel, with a few men only, generally of Hindoo origin. The *Donys* profit of the south-west monsoon to make a yearly voyage to Calcutta, with their sails set from the moment of their departure till their arrival. They set out again with the north-east monsoon. Without these precautions they never could keep the sea, from the great ignorance of their sailors and the clumsiness of their vessels. These sailors too are unable to stand damp weather; it enervates them to such a degree, that even the Mussulmans, who are tolerable seamen in the hot climates, sink under it, and become unfit for service.

Commentary: The *donī* (Tamil, *toṅi*; Telugu, *donī*) is a common boat on South India's Coromandel coast and in Sri Lanka and is variously described as both small and large. *Hobson-Jobson* identifies it as "a small native vessel" that, as both early accounts and etymology suggests, evolved from a dugout.[1] In the first volume of *The Journal of the Royal Asiatic Society of Great Britain and Ireland*, Edye, formerly His Majesty's Master Shipwright in Ceylon, describes it as "a huge vessel of ark-like form, about seventy feet long, twenty feet broad, and twelve feet deep; with a flat bottom or keep part, which at the broadest place is seven feet" and, confirming Solvyns's judgment, "the whole equipment of these rude vessels, as well as their construction, is the most coarse and un-seaworthy that I have ever seen."[2] Solvyn's donī is considerably smaller, however. In a preliminary drawing, from an album assembled by his widow, Solvyns penciled in its dimensions as 36 feet in length and 12 feet in breadth.

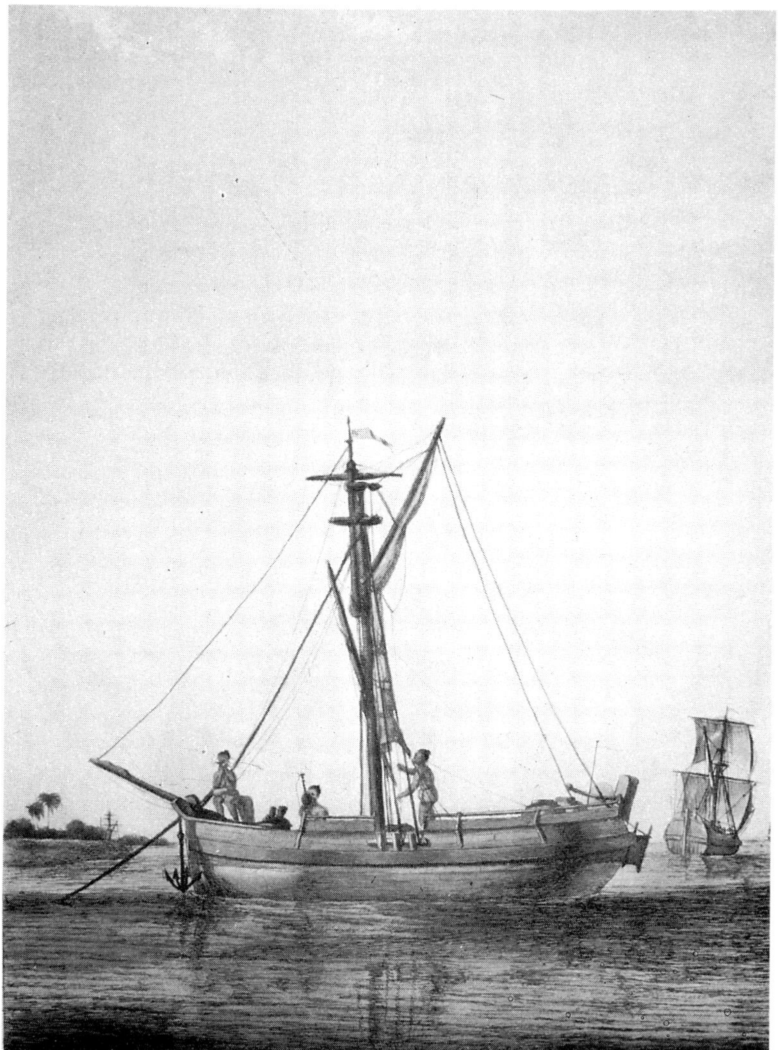

DONĪ. Paris: III.3.2.

In his note to the original drawing, Solvyns described the *donī* as "A vessel with two or three masts, but commonly with one, [as] represented in the drawing.[3] The Dony appears an ill constructed clumsy vessel; they are employed generally in carrying salt from Balasore and the coast."

European influence is evident in many donīs, as those portrayed here by Solvyns, and boats of this type, confined to coastal navigation between Bengal and the Coromandel, were disparaged as "pariahs" by French sailors. These boats, Deloche writes, "had a square stern with a high poop, a rigging of European influence with a large mast bearing a fore-and-aft sail, topsail and sometimes a top gallant," and were built at Coringa (Korangi) on the Godavari coast of what is today Andhra Pradesh. "Almost all of these boats had a bad reputation among European sailors, who considered them to be badly built, weak and lacking in stability because of their light water draft. Their rigging was judged inefficient, not allowing the boats to venture any great distance from the coast, for fear of being carried off to open seas by the south-westernly winds."[4]

NOTES

1 323.

2 Edye, 13. Kerchove, in the *International Maritime Dictionary*, 213, identifies the "doney" as a coaster on the east coast of India, with a length of 70 to 100 feet, a breadth of 20 to 21 feet, and depth of 12 to 14 feet. It has a keelless flat bottom and a fore- and afterbody of similar form.

3 Admiral Smyth, 257, states that these "unshapely" vessels have only one mast, but according to Kerchove, 213, the rig consists of one, two, or three masts, with lateen or gaff sails. Headsails are carried on a bowsprit with huge jibboom.

4 Deloche, 2:185-86.

15. Jāliyā Ḍiṅgi

Calcutta: Sec. VIII, No. 7. A Jell-a Dingee, or Fishing Boat.
Paris: III.3.3. Jellee-a Dingee.

This is a very light and well-built boat, used for fishing. The pilot of the *Jellee-a* sits high at the top of his boat, and steers it with an oar which he frequently manages with his feet, while his hands are employed with the hooka which he is constantly smoking. They are of different size according to the nature of the fishery; the topsy (mango fish, described in the New Dictionary of natural history),[1] the shad. For this latter, which is so abundant that five and twenty or thirty are sometimes to be had for a roupee, there are a vast number of boats of an extraordinary length, which carry five or six fishermen. These boats take also large quantities of prawns, which are eaten by the people with great avidity. The Mugs[2] and Malays keep them till they are putrid, and blend them with salt into a paste, which has a very strong smell, and is put up in jars and small pots for use. Some fishermen remain often four months together in their boats without leaving them. It seems that the *Jellee-a* has served as a model for all the other boats which are used in Hindoostan.

Commentary: Hornell provides a similar description for the jāliyā (or jeli) ḍiṅgi to that of Solvyns, noting that "they differ considerabably in detail and proportion and have their special local names, often given however not because of difference in form but merely because of the kind of net used from them. . . ."[3]

"In form and construction all varieties of he *jalia dinghi* are admirable and exactly suited to contend with the strong currents and tides of the Ganges and its branches within tidal influence. Its rounded bottom, the high sheer of stem and stern and narrow build make it easy to handle in a tide way; they are lively craft and require considerable skill in handling."[4] Reflecting a variety of traditions in boat-building technology, used simultaneously, as in many boats of Bengal, ḍiṅgi construction is eclectic.

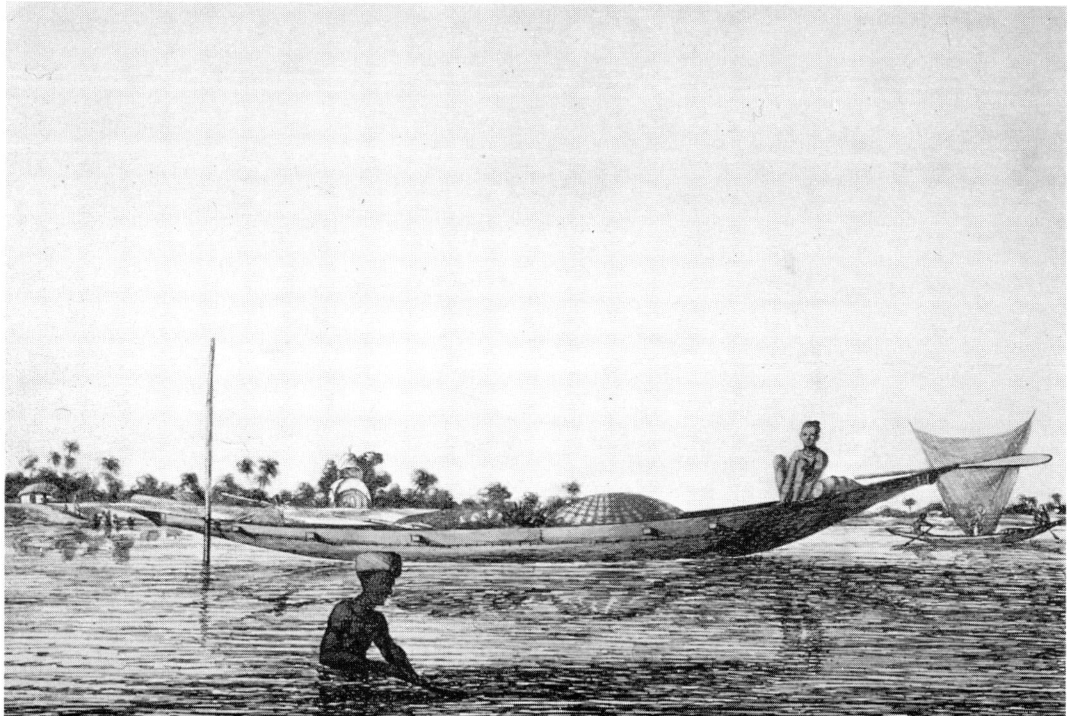

JĀLIYĀ DIṄGI. Paris: III.3.3.

Fishermen in the jāliyā ḍiṅgi in the background hoist the net.

NOTES

1 The volume to which Solvyns refers is William Frederick Martyn, *A New Dictionary of Natural History*, 2 vols. London: Harrison & Co., 1785. Solvyns portrays the tapsī (tapassī) fish, in *Les Hindoûs*, IV.10.6. Flavorful and highly prized as a delicacy, it appears in Calcutta markets with the onset of the hot season, when the mangoes ripen. Thus, it is often called a "mango fish."

2 On the "Mugs," or Maghs, see Commentary on Kośā (Pl. 28).

3 "The Boats of the Ganges," 182.

4 Ibid., 183.

16. Saraṅgā

Calcutta: Sec. IX, No. 10. A Scringee,—being an Ek-gachee [ekṭhā, Pl. 17] with the addition of some Planks on each side.
Paris: III.3.4. Seringee.

The *Seringee* resembles the last boat which we have described, and differs from it only by having a few more planks. Some of them are of a great length, and these are generally used in the *sunderbunds,* or very close woods, which are infested by tigers and other ferocious animals. This species of *Seringee* is manned by *banbuyties,* a sort of banditti, who accost the vessels they meet in the evening, under pretext of asking to light their fire. Three of four only of their crew appear; the remainder are hid under the sails and mats. If they perceive that the vessel is too strongly manned to be attacked, they follow their course; if on the contrary they feel sufficiently strong, they board it and carry off all the cargo, and not unfrequently throw the passenger into the river. The *Chaukys,* a sort of boat very well manned, give chase to these river pirates, and punish them severely as often as they catch them. The *Seringee* represented in the engraving is of the smaller sort, and has paddles instead of oars. It follows a larger vessel, and is laden with leather jars filled with fish oil. That in the distance is one of the *banbuyties.* The view represents one of the *sunderbunds* which we have just mentioned.

Commentary: The saraṅgā is the general term for cargo-carrying dugouts in eastern Bengal, and similar dugouts, sometimes with variations in size and and form, are found throughout the region, each with distinct names, such as ekṭhā (Pl. 17), ḍoṅga (Pl. 18) and śālti. Greenhill writes that saraṅgās "are cut from single logs, hollowed out until only the equivalent of a thin planking . . . is left" and then built up on the sides with planks, which are secured to the dugout by split bamboo stitches. The seam is caulked.[1] Jansen, in *Country Boats of Bangladesh,* describes the "sharonga" as "a sea-going boat. . . , both small and medium-sized, used in fishing as well as transport."[2] In his

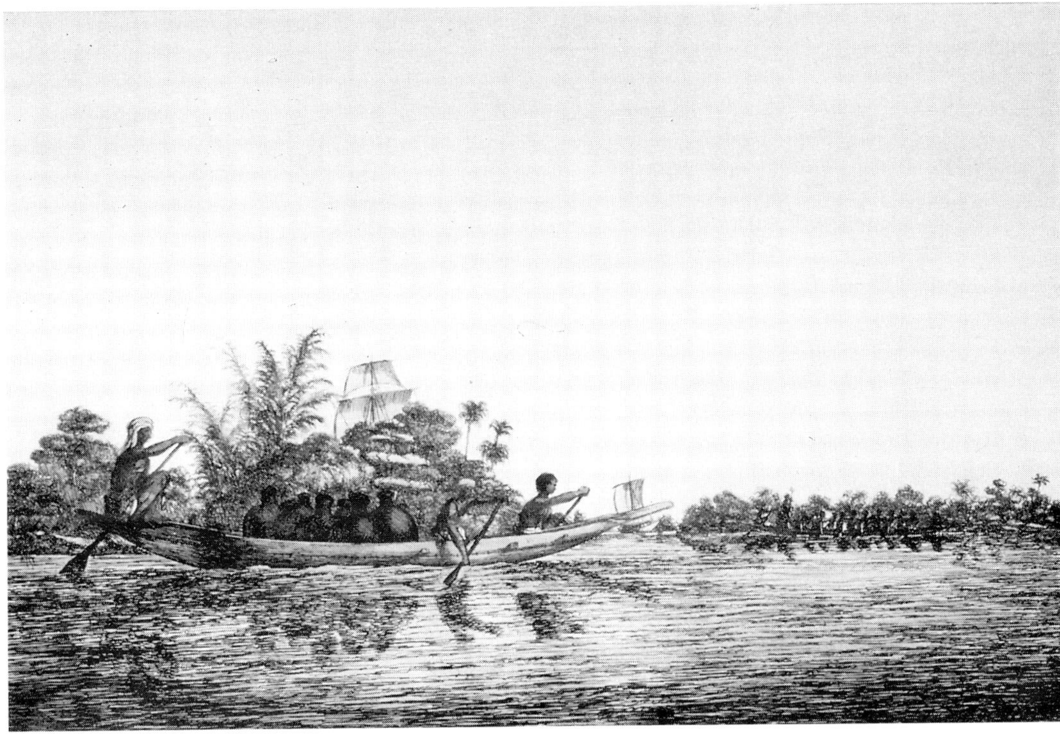

SARAṄGĀ. Paris: III.3.4.

note to the original drawing, Solvyns indicates that "some are as large as 200 or 300 maunds." They are, he writes, used with paddles, as portrayed in the etching.

That spellings and pronunciations vary for the names of boats in Bengal—not to mention transliterations—is surely evident in the words for this boat. Solvyns gives three different transliterations, and it appears elsewhere, without diacriticals, as saranga (Greenhill), sharonga (Jansen), and in sources cited by Jansen as sarangi and haranga.[3]

Solvyns refers to *banbuyties,* whom he describes as "a sort of banditti." Bandits—*dacoits* in common Indian parlance—were widespead in Bengal, especially in the Sunderbunds, the area of intersecting channels, swampy islands, and jungles of the lower Ganges delta.[4] In the early days of British rule, these "night-hawks of the river" operated at night in long and narrow many-oared boats "to plunder inland villages or, gaining one of the main rivers, would attack the slow-moving heavy cargo boats and merchant vessels, robbing and slaying with impunity, disappearing again, as swifty as they had come, to their lairs in the riverine labyrinth of the delta."[5]

Perhaps Solvyns here portrays the Sunderbund channel that Europeans in the seventeenth and eighteenth centuries called "Rogues's River." "It was so called from being frequented by the Arakan Rovers, sometimes Portuguese vagabonds, sometimes native Muggs,[6] whose vessels lay in this creek watching their opportunity to plunder craft going up and down the Hoogly [Hugli]."[7]

Solvyns identifies the saraṅgā in the distance of his portrayal as manned by "banbuyties." In the Calcutta etching, the boat is only sketchily evident, but for the Paris edition, Solvyns changes the composition by shifting the boat of the foreground to one side and, in the background, detailing the pirate saraṅgā with a dozen boatmen. A large, square-rigged merchantman, the sails of which are seen above the trees, may represent its pray.

Solvyns's *chauky* is probably a guard boat, taking its name from *caukī,* Hindustani for "guard station."

NOTES

1 111-13. Also see Hornell, "The Boats of the Ganges," 179-80; and Deloche, 2:156-58.

2 80.

3 Ibid.

4 *Hobson-Jobson*, "Decoit," 290. See Marshall, *Bengal: The British Bridgehead*, 98, on decoity in Bengal in the late eighteenth and early nineteenth centuries. On the Sunderbunds, see *Hobson-Jobson*, 869; Deloche, 2: 122-23.

5 Hornell, "The Boats of Bengal," 183-84.

6 On the Maghs, see Commentary on Kośā (Pl. 28).

7 *Hobson-Jobson*, 765.

17. Ekṭhā

Calcutta: Sec. IX, No. 9. An Ek-gachee,—a Canoe made from the trunk of a tree.
Paris: III.3.5. Ekgachee.

The *Ekgachees,* like the *Seringees,* are a sort of canoe, that is to say, a bark cut out of the trunk of a tree. They serve as lumber-boats, and follow larger vessels which carry commodities, particularly rice, to the bazars. The oar of the *Ekgachee* is a long bambou fastened to a small board. At some distance from it I have represented another little bark belonging also to a larger vessel. This is flatbottomed, its planks are joined by *rattans,* or small bambous. The *Ekgachee* generally carry three *Dandys,* two of whom work while the other rests and smokes; they make three meals a day of coarse rice, their ordinary food, to which they sometimes add vegetables and fish. They are constantly smoking a bad sort of tobacco, and at night, after their last meal, they sit round the *Magie* [*mājjī*] or pilot, and amuse themselves by telling stories till they fall asleep. They lie in the open air, with a bit of cloth for their only covering: in winter they get under the sail: one of them is obliged to keep watch. They sometimes, as a pastime, play on the *sittar*[1] or some other of the instruments which we have already described.

Commentary: According to Hornell, the dugout canoe, called ḍoṅga (Pl. 18) in Bengal, is known as ekṭhā in Bihar, "a name evidently given in reference to this kind of boat being formed out of a simple log or tree trunk." Such boats, he writes, are usually from 10 to 15 feet in length, with a breadth of two feet or more, and with about the same depth[2]—a description that corresponds to Solvyns's portrayal, but the ekṭhā depicted is clearly distinct in form from the ḍoṅga and bears greater similarity, as Solvyns notes, to the saraṅgā (Pl. 16).

The word "ekgachee" (*ekgāchi*) appears in no dictionary (nor does the "agacha" of Solvyns's note to the drawing), but seems descriptive of the dugout—*ek* (one) + *gach* (tree).

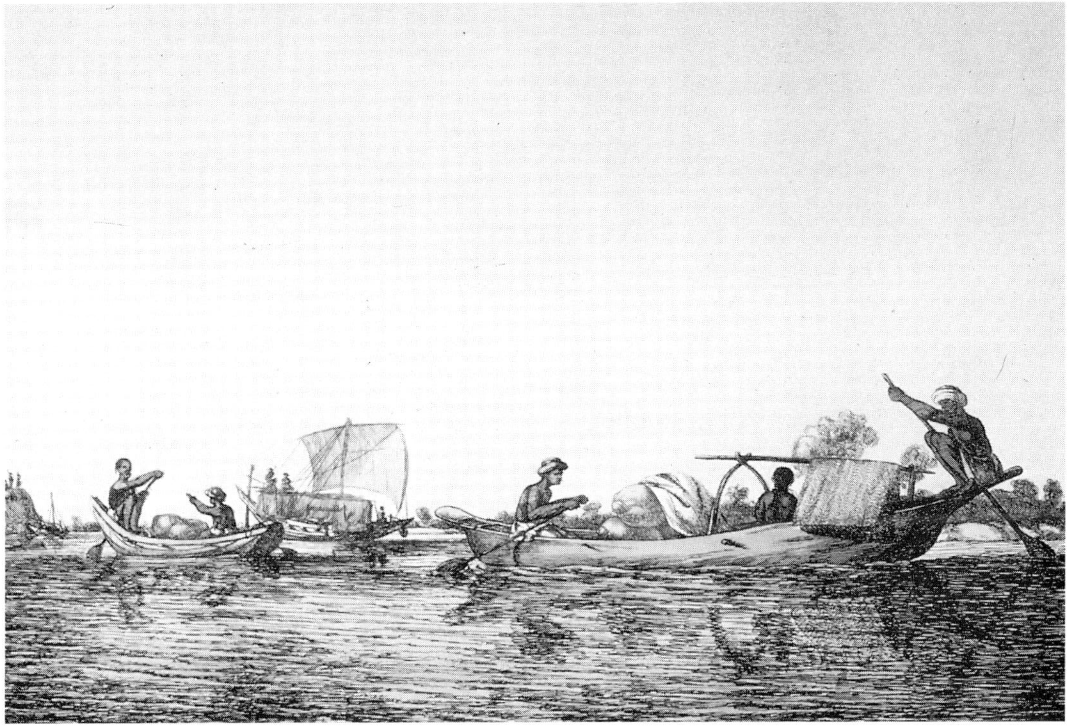

EKṬHĀ. Paris: III.3.5.

In the Calcutta etching, the boat is centered in the foreground and fills the print, but for the Paris etching, Solvyns moves the ekṭhā to the right and widens the perspective, adding a small dugout and a pāṭeli (Pl. 22) in the background to the left.

NOTES

1 The instrument is portrayed by Solvyns in Calcutta: Sec. XI. No. 4, and Paris: II.7.2. It is included in Hardgrave and Slawek, 45-49.

2 "The Boats of the Ganges," 177, 179. Also see Deloche, 2:256-58.

18. Ḍoṅga

Calcutta: Sec. VIII, No. 10. A Gunga,—a small bark made out of a toddy tree, and used for fishing, &c.
Paris: III.3.6. Gunga.

This is a very small boat hollowed out from the trunk of a tree, and takes its name of *Gunga*, or shell, from its form. It is used on the lakes and tanks, for spreading fishing-nets and other purposes. Many different sorts of *Gungas* are represented in the print. The view is a saltwater lake, about a league from Calcutta. This lake is surrounded by *sunderbands,* where the Hindoos sometimes go to cut wood, but never without great risk, from the quantity of tigers with which these close woods are infested. Allured by the prospect of a trifling gain, to brave this danger, they approach the borders of the woods in large boats, offer up sacrifices on their landing, and light fires with a great deal of noise to frighten off the tigers. They are sometimes successful, and cut wood enough to lade all their boats, which they sell for a tolerable profit at Calcutta; but it frequently happens that they never return, and it is then certain that they have been devoured by the wild beasts. As a memorial of such misfortunes, they plant in the earth an oar bearing a *cudgeri* [*khicuṛī*] or earthen pot. Many of these monuments are seen at a little distance from each other: a melancholy proof of the frequency of these accidents.

Commentary: Solvyns's "gunga" (*ghonghā* 'shell' in Hindustani) may be a local usage, but, more likely, his ear failed him, for the boat Solvyns depicts is, in Bengali, called a ḍoṅga, defined in the *Etymological Dictionary of Bengali* as a "trough-like bark."[1]

James Hornell writes that "Dug-out canoes, called *donga* in Bengal, and *ekhta* in Bihar, are seen everywhere in the shallow tributaries of the Ganges. . . . Commonest of all [illustrated by Hornell and portrayed by Solvyns] is the little dug-out made from the lower end of the stem of the Palmyra palm. . . . The entire butt end of the tree is used together with 8 or 10 feet of the cylindrical stem

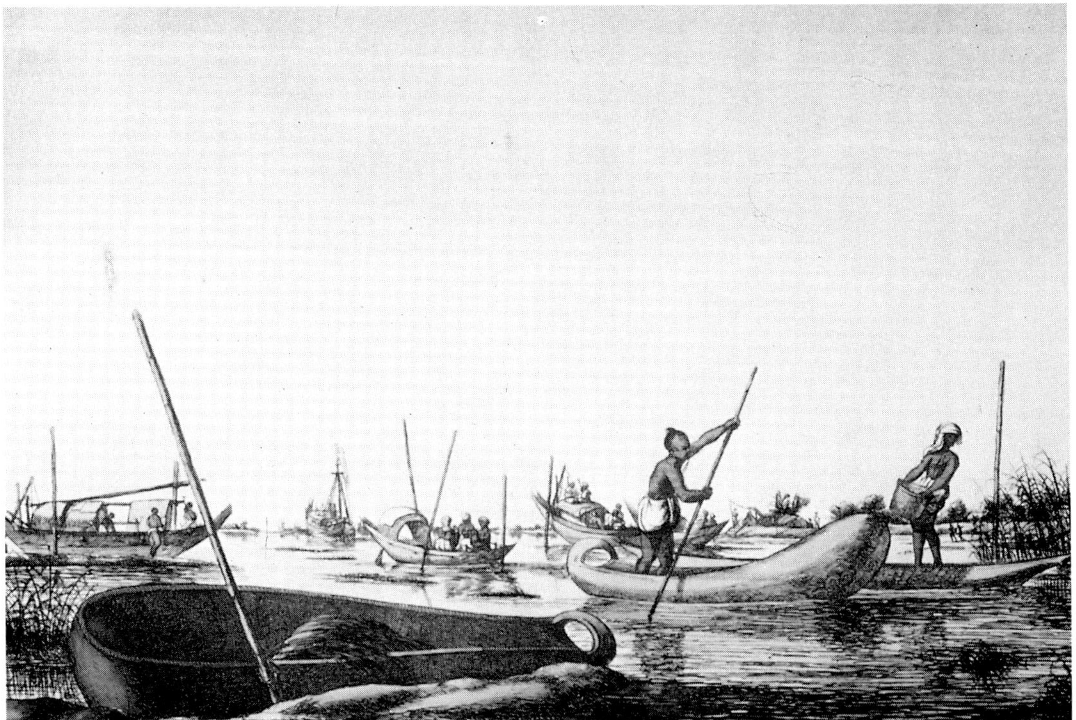

ḌOṄGA. Paris: III.3.6.

above. The butt end of this palm is unusally bulbous, and when hollowed out gives a wide roomy cavity where a considerable quantity of goods can be stored, or several passengers accommodated if they sit close together at the bottom."[2] The trunk end of the ḍoṅga "is sealed with a mud wall or a fragment of the palm's soft interior. . . ."[3]

These dugouts "were commonly employed over a large part of the watercourses by the peasants to go from village to village, to cross inundated paddies, or to transport their produce to neighbouring markets."[4]

In the print, the single boatman poles the ḍoṅga with a long bamboo. Most boats in Bengal carry such poles for use when unable to row or sail.

NOTES

1 Sukumar Sen, 377. The word *ḍoṅga* is also used for a ḍiṅgi fashioned of the shell-like bark of the banana tree.

2 "The Boats of the Ganges," 177. Also see Hornell, *Water Transport*, 190.

3 Greenhill, *Boats and Boatmen of Pakistan*, 111.

4 Deloche, 2:156-58.

19. Balasore Roads

Paris: III.4.1. View of Ballasore Roads.

Ballasore is an open road, and offers nothing but the sea to the view: the weather must be very clear to discover the distant point of Palmyre, the highlands of Piply, or the roof of some pagoda. It is frequented by different sorts of vessels, and particularly by large ships from Bombay, Surate, and other parts of the western coast, with moorish crews. There are also several vessels from the Ganges, called *Schooners,* very well fitted out, and able to make a voyage to Europe: their pilots are very skilfull. The anchorage in the road is good; but these vessels prefer remaining under sail, to keep a better look-out for ships, which it is their business to pilot into the entrance of the *Ougly* [Hugli], and for which they are constantly plying in the roads of Ballasore. This entrance is full of danger: and, to avoid it, an experienced pilot is absolutely necessary. Besides the man who takes charge of the ship, another is employed constantly in throwing the lead, and crying out the depth of water and quality of the bottom, while a pilot vessel precedes the ship at a little distance, and makes signals to him who steers it.

The print represents several different sorts of vessels, with a pilot schooner stationed in the road.

Commentary: On the north coast of Orissa, Balasore (Baleshwar), 125 miles south of Calcutta, provided sheltered anchorage for Indiamen awaiting favorable winds—and an experienced pilot—to take them up the Hugli river or for the transfer of goods and passengers from the larger ships to sloops (Pl. 31) or other boats for the trip upriver.

Solvyns writes that the pilot vessels were "called *Schooners*" and that in the etching he represents "a pilot schooner stationed in the road," but the print depicts no schooner-rigged vessels. Schooners, built in India, had earlier been used by the Bengal Pilot Service, though it is unlikely that they were in service in Solvyns's time.[1] Pilot boats,

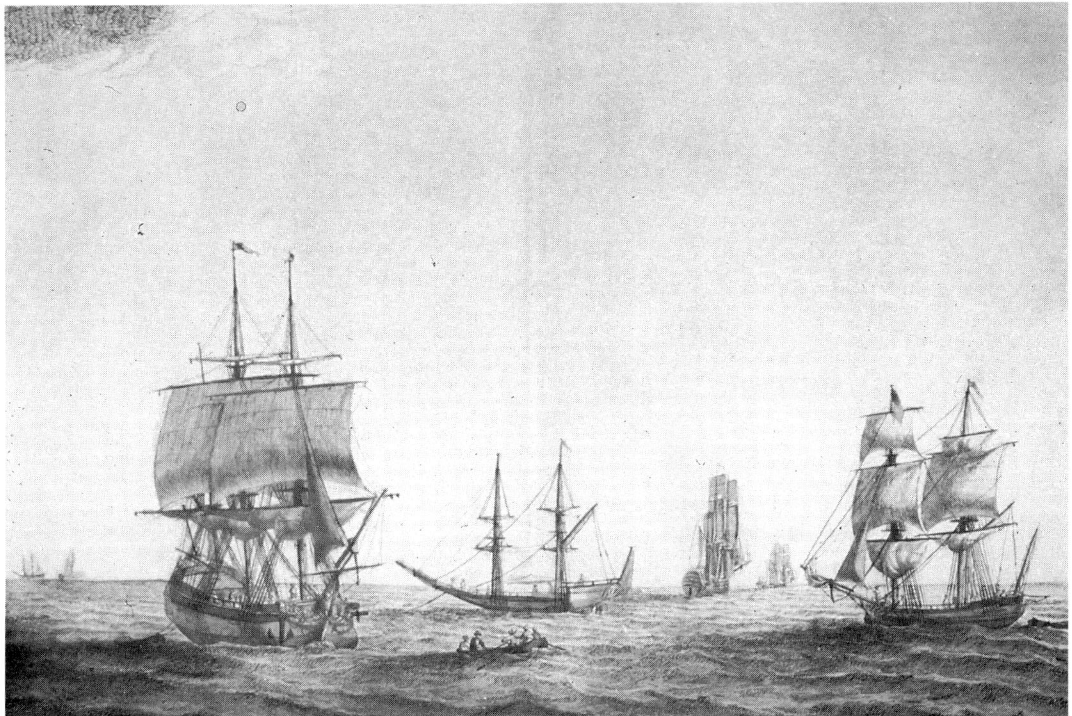

BALASORE ROADS. Paris: IV.1. (double plate)

typically brigs from the late eighteenth century, apparently continued to be called "schooners," and, indeed, the term was often used loosely to describe any small fast vessel suitable for the river, but Solvyns, trained in Europe as a marine painter, would surely have been familiar with the schooner proper. The term "schooner" was first applied to a fore-and-aft rigged, two-masted vessel in New England in the early eighteenth century, though other craft of similar rigging dated from 1600 in Holland.[2]

The print is not included in the Calcutta edition, and, as in his depiction of *Vessels of All Sorts* (Pl. 36), Solvyns presents a composite, using his own drawings from India, as with the grab, but also taking images from other sources. What then does Solvyns portray in his *View of Ballasore Roads*? Daniel Finamore, curator of marine painting at Salem's Peabody Essex Museum, identifies the central ship as a grab (Pl. 20), with a square-rigged foremast and squaresail-main top, fore-and-aft spanker, thus making it a standard brig rig. It has a very sharp bow and an unconventional construction at the stern, perhaps a passenger compartment.

On the left is a full-rigged ship of standard European type, though hardly graceful in design. It is old-fashioned for Solvyns's time, as indicated by its early eighteenth century spritsail yard, and Finamore suggests it likely that Solvyns copied the image from an older European print or painting. To the center right is a full-rigged European ship, and on the far right is a standard brig of the 1790-1810 era.

Balasore had been an early European commercial center, with an English factory established in 1633,[3] but with the rise of Calcutta, it came to be the center for pilot services. River pilots boarded the smaller ships to steer them upsteam through the trecherous sandbars of the Hugli to safe harbor at Diamond Harbor, 41 miles south of Calcutta, or on to Calcutta itself.[4] For the Indiamen able to proceed upriver, pilot boats typically led the way into the Hugli, between the "sandheads"—shoals that stretched out from the mouth of the river like fingers—but, as decreed by the East India Company Board of Directors in 1700, ships of more than 400 tons burden were to anchor in Balasore Roads or at Kijari (Kedgeree), at the mouth of the Hugli, and their passengers and goods were to be transferred to smaller boats for transport to Calcutta.[5]

Often the last leg of the trip for passagers, from Diamond Point or Kulpi (Anglo-Indian "Culpee," a few miles below it on the Hugli) to Calcutta, was by bājrā (Pl. 5) or, more grandly, by fīlcehrā (Pl. 3).[6]

Palmyras Point, to which Solvyns refers, is a promontory below Balasore that served as a landmark for vessels from the south, and it was just past this headland that ships encountered the pilots that would lead them into the shifting channels of Hugli.[7] Pipli, north of Balasore, had been a center of Portuguese, Dutch, and English trade in the mid-seventeenth century, but by Solvyns's time, much of the coastal town had washed away.[8]

NOTES

1 Maritime historian Anne Bulley records that several schooners were built in the Bombay dockyard for the Bengal Pilot Service between 1753 and 1776, but they were apparently not altogether satisfactory, and in the 1780s and 1790s, four brigs and a snow were built for the Pilot Service—but no schooners. Personal communication, January 22, 1998. See Bulley, *The Bombay Country Ships.*

2 MacGregor, 13. Early schooners were two-masted, and by Solvyns's time, some carried three masts. From the mid-nineteenth century, schooners ranged from two to six masts. Also see Kerchove, 629-30.

3 On the history of Balasore, see Hunter, *A Statistical Account of Bengal,* 18:280-83; Walter Hamilton, *A Geographical, Statistical, and Historical Description of Hindostan and Adjacent Countries,* 2:37; Deloche, 2:116; and Tripati, 156-57.

4 See, for example, the description by Father Matteo Ripa in 1709, quoted Nair, *Calcutta in the 18th Century,* 19. The various points of the river are described in "Early Charts and Topography of the Hugli River," Note by Henry Yule, in Hedges, 3:197-220. On Diamond Harbor, see Commentary on Sloop (Pl. 31).

5 Marshman, in Alok Ray, 181. Deloche, in his account of water transport in India, 2:117-23, provides detailed information on the Hugli estuary and coastal fluvial navigation of the region. For a map of the area, from Palmyras Point up the Hugli to Calcutta, see Jean Sutton, 117, and description, 118. On the pilot service, also see Nilmani Mukherjee, 4-6, 26, 30.

6 Firminger's note on "Culpee," Stanhope, 29, vi.

7 Walter Hamilton, *East India Gazetteer,* 2:407.

8 See Walter Hamilton, *A Geographical, Statistical, and Historical Description of Hindostan and Adjacent Countries,* 1:152; Milbourn, 250; Deloche, 2:116; and Tripati, 157-58.

20. Grab

Calcutta: Sec. IX, No. 1. A Grab:—a method of building peculiar to Bombay. Paris: III.4.2. Grab.

This is a ship with three masts, a pointed prow, and a bowsprit, as is represented in the print: its crew consists of a *Nicodar* [*nākhodā*][1] or captain, and a few *Clashies* [*khālasī*] or Moorish sailors, generally of a very robust frame. The *Grabs* are built at Bombay, where it appears that navigation was brought to some degree of perfection at a very early period. In this part of India too the teck [teak] is found, a resinous tree on which they say that the sea-worm has no effect. This is used for the sides and ribs; but the keel, and in general all that is under water, is made of saul [ṣāl],[2] very heavy wood which the Hindoos look upon as incorruptible; and in effect this timber remains sometimes for ages uninjured, but at other rots almost as soon as it is cut. In their most ancient temples there are beams of this wood as solid and as fresh as if they had been but just put up.

The pointed prow which distinguishes the *Grab* belongs to the Hindoo construction, and is not met with in any other country. The Portugese have imitated it in their India ships. Sometimes also the poops of the Hindoo vessels are very high, as they were formerly in our European seas.

Commentary: "Grab" is an Anglo-Indian word (near obsolete by the late nineteenth century) from the Arabic *ghurāb*, literally "raven," applied to a kind of galley used along the coasts of the Indian Oceans. The grab draws little water, is broad in proportion to its length, and varies in size from 150 to 500 tons burden. It has two, sometimes three masts that are square-rigged, and it has an elongated bow. Various descriptions specify that it does not have a bowsprit,[3] but Solvyns's grab does have a bowsprit as well as the less common three masts. The masts, with European rigging, carry a lower sail and top sail, with a flag atop. There is a spanker, or gaff-headed sail, at the stern.[4] Solvyns's portrayal presents an interesting amalgamation of

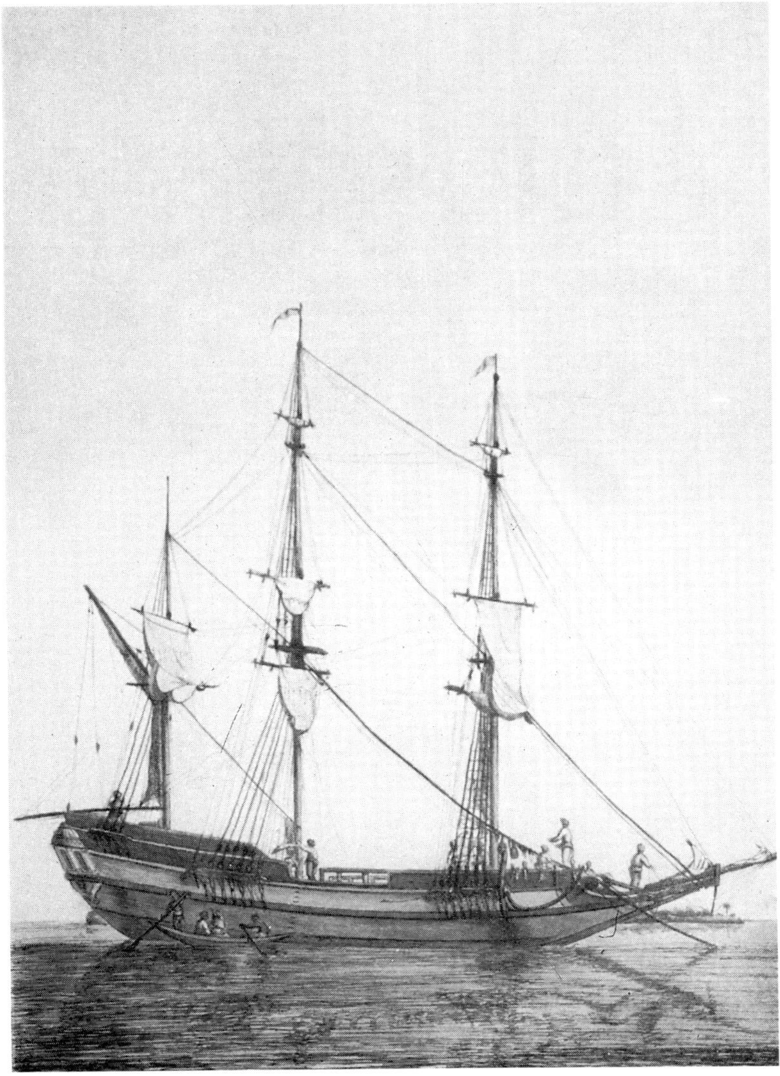

GRAB. Paris: IV.2.

sophisticated Western rigging on an Eastern hull of specialized local design.

In his note to the original drawing, Solvyns writes that the "mode of building" seen in the grab has been long used in India. They are, he continues, "commonly 250 to 300 tons burden rigged as a brig; or snow,[5] but some have three masts [as he portrays here] and are of 800 tons."

Many grabs which sailed out of Arabia and the Persian Gulf and others from the western coast of India could well have had "Moorish" crews, but "clashy" (*khālasī*) is a general term applied to native sailors and a variety of servants or workmen, as Solvyns portrays in a separate etching.[6]

NOTES

1 Persian for a "skipper," corrupted as *nākhodā*, *nacoda*, etc. *OED*; *Hobson-Jobson*, 612; Lewis, 173.
2 See "saul-wood," *Hobson-Jobson*, 798.
3 *Hobson-Jobson*, 391-92; *OED*.
4 See Deloche, 2:193.
5 A snow is a small brig-like sailing ship, carrying a main and fore mast and a supplementary trysail mast close behind the main mast. *OED*.
6 Calcutta: Sec. II, No. 22; Paris: IV.3.6.

21. Bangles

Calcutta: Sec. IX, No. 11. A Bangles,—a large rice boat of from 2 to 4000 maunds.
Paris: III.4.3. Bangles.

The *Bangles* are incontestably the largest boats in the rivers of Hindoostan: some of them carry four or even five thousand *maunds* of rice; a *maund* is worth 75 pounds. They have a roof of thatch [*chāuni*] to protect the *Magie* [*mājhī*, captain] and the sailors or *Dandies,* who are almost always Hindoos. The merchant has a sort of cabin in the aft of the vessel. The masts of the *Bangles* are of an enormous size, and consist of several bambous fastened together. The *Bangles* in the print is placed so as to shew the whole of its form. At a distance are seen several boats of this kind under sail. The poop is generally covered with ornaments in brass and wreaths of flowers, like all the Hindoo vessels. The owners of these boats make but one trip in the year, setting out in the rainy season, and returning home before the great droughts. The sailors make cordage and other necessary articles, during the passage.

Commentary: Solvyns's term *Bangles* does not appear as a boat in dictionaries and would seem to derive from a generic *Bāṅgāli*, "belonging to Bengal."[1]

Solvyns states that the boats have a mast of enormous size, as portrayed in the Calcutta etching. For the Paris etching, however, Solvyns took down the mast, although the *Bangles* in the distance are depicted with mast raised and at sail. Although anchored, the boat in the foreground of the etching is shown with a wooden grapnel anchor on the side.

NOTE

1 Sukumar Sen, 628.

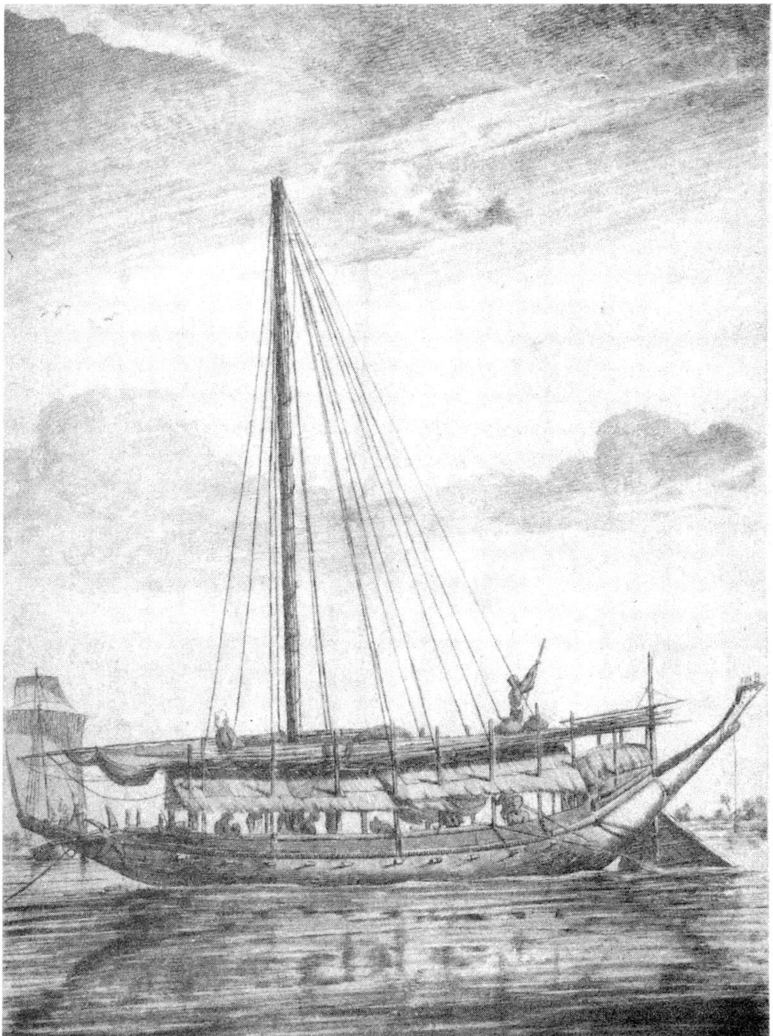

BANGLES. Calcutta: Sec. IX, No. 11.

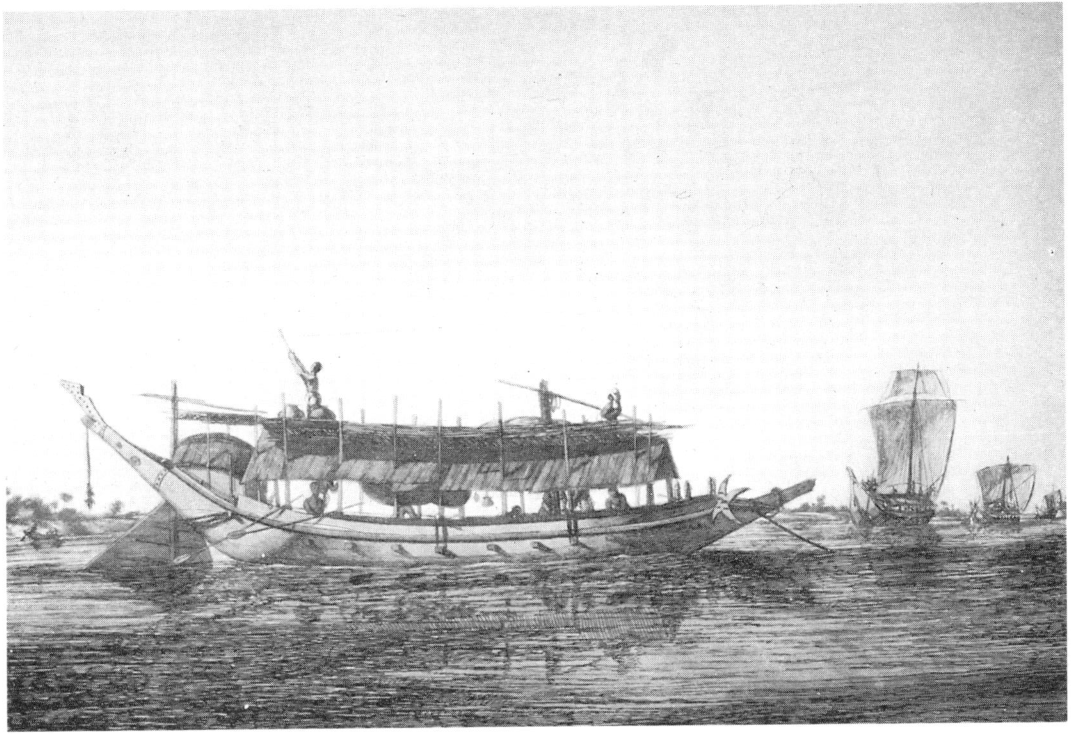

BANGLES. Paris: III.4.3.

22. Pāṭeli

Calcutta: Sec. IX, No. 7. A Pataily,—a flat clinker built boat from the Provinces of Behar and Benares.
Paris: III.4.4. Pataily.

This is the name of a boat very common in the provinces of Behar and Benares, but seldom seen in the other parts of Hindoostan. It is flat, except at the two ends, which are a little raised. It is the worst of all Hindoo vessels, and made of planks laid over each other without being worked up or planed: the outside is gross and without ornament. Instead of masts, the *Pataily* frequently has but a *bambou,* and some *gonies* [*gonī,* gunny] for sails. It has a covering of thatch like the other lumber-boats, but is in general so ill constructed that it is five or six times longer getting up the river, and it is even surprising to see so poor a vessel undertake long voyages. Its general lading is rice, for it is seldom trusted with a more valuable cargo, though I have sometimes seen it freighted with other merchandise.

Commentary: The pāṭeli is a large flat-bottomed boat of the Ganges. Upcountry, it is known as a katrā, and Solvyns provides a separate print (Pl. 23) for the boat under that name. Solvyns expresses little confidence in the vessel, but a hundred years earlier, Thomas Bowrey thought these boats, which carried saltpetre and grain, of "Exeeding Strength." "They are built very Strong, by reason of the most impetuous Eddies they meet with in some places, that force them many times Upon one Shoale or Other. . . ."[1]

Prinsep, in 1830, describes the pāṭeli as a "baggage boat." It is clinker-built, that is, with overlapping planks, and "its great breadth gives it a very light draught of water, and renders it fittest for the cotton and other up-country products, which require little better than a dray and secure raft to float them down the stream."[2] Pāṭelis vary in size, usually in the range of 35 tons burden, but occasionally double that size, and they carry grain, salt, cotton, and other produce.[3] The boat, writes Colesworthy Grant, is an "unwieldy-

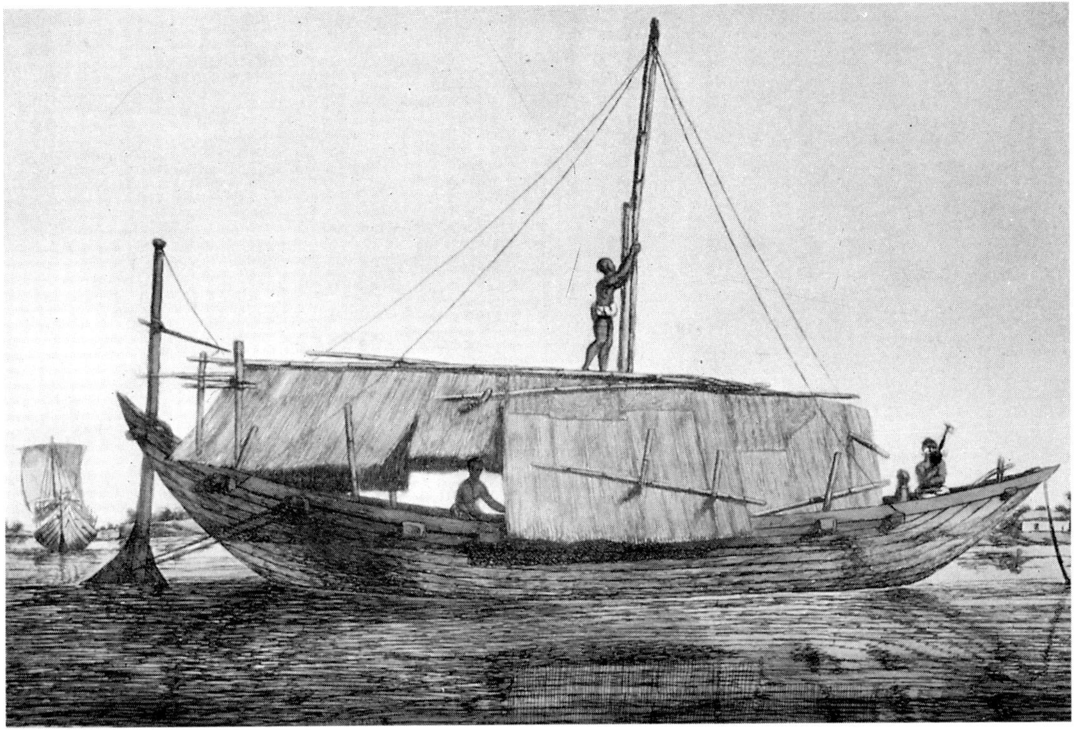

PĀṬELI. Paris: III.4.4.

looking piece of rusticity" and is used by some Europeans as a baggage boat. "Families in middling or narrow circustances journey-ing to the upper provinces, avail themselves of boats of this description. . . ."[4]

The pāṭeli "is manned by ten or twelve boatmen,—each man—when there is no wind to bring the sail into use—standing up on the bamboo platform or roof, and labouring at an enormous bamboo oar, full eighteen feet in length, with a broad round blade at its extremity, like a baker's peel, with which it is impossible for more than one stroke to be made in about two minutes!"[5]

Admiral Paris' Native Boats, 1841, provides a detailed description:

> The transportation of produce from the upper regions of Bengal requires strong boats. The largest of this type of vessel is the "patilé". Some are planked and nailed, while others are clinker-built, with wooden pins joining the planks to the framework. Some have a flat, vertical rear, a very slanting front, flattened out at the bottom, and lateral planks pinned to the sides. The upper part of the side, which is made from several pinned planks, is covered with a large projecting plank, on whch a man can stand to punt. Sometimes, other planks are positioned on the ends of the beams for the same purpose. The rudder, which is positioned at the side, is triangular.
>
> These boats vary in length from 12 to 20 meters. They all carry a large cabin made from reeds tied with twine, and covered with a coconut palm thatch. Through this go posts, which support cross-beams laid with such a haphazard assortment of planks and poles that only Indians can walk across them.
>
> The sails, supported by bamboo poles, are very small.
>
> Some of the large "patilés" from Calcutta, which have their planking held together by cramp-irons, have rounder lines, very similar to those of "bauléas" [bhāuliyā, Pl. 6]. Their rear, which is pointed and very high, is made from a single piece of wood, which is stronger than planking. They have a framework, and projecting beams, but never any decking. They carry enormous cabins, which are covered by a platform which is as long as the boat itself. The lightness of their construction, and their flat lines allow them to carry sizeable loads, and they are especially suited to the transportation of cotton.[6]

Solvyns portrays the pāṭeli broadside, with a background view of the boat head on with sail.

NOTES

1 Bowrey, 225. Also see 229.
2 48, with illustration in Appendix A4.
3 *Hobson-Jobson*, 687-88; Hunter, *A Statistical Account of Bengal*, 1: 33; and Deloche, 2:161.
4 *Rural Life in Bengal*, 6, with a small engraving of a "putelee."
5 Ibid., 25. The "great steering paddle" on the cargo boats is described by Hornell in "The Origins and Ethnological Significance of Indian Boat Designs," 189, and in "The Boats of the Ganges," 192-93.
6 35-37.

23. Katrā

Calcutta: Sec. IX, No. 8. A Kautry,—from the Northern Provinces of Hindostan, differing little from a Pataily with the head and stern reversed. Paris: III.4.5. Kautry.

The *Kautry* is higher in the prow and lower astern than the *Pataily* [pāṭeli, Pl. 22] from which it is distinguished by this difference of construction. The northern countries of Hindoostan employ a great number of *Kautrys* in conveying their produce to Calcutta, from whence they frequently return with the troops which are to be cantoned in the upper districts, or attend the *Pinnaces* [Pl. 2] and *Budgerows* [bājrā, Pl. 5] going to Lucknow or elsewhere, as baggage boats, with the kitchen and provisions. The Hindoos who come with the *Kautrys* are more robust than those of Bengal, speak a language of their own, and sometimes the true Hindoo tongue [Sanskrit]. They are three or four months getting up the river, during which time their patience must be equal to their exertions. There can be no relaxation in their efforts to overcome the force of the currents, against which they have to hawl up a very heavy boat, and escape the danger of the squalls in which, notwithstanding all their labour and perseverance, many of them perish.

Commentary: Solvyns notes a slight difference in construction between the katrā and the pāṭeli, but both are flat-bottomed and clinker-built. The difference is essentially in the name. The boat is known as a katrā in the upper Ganges area and as pāṭeli in the mid-Ganges region of Bihar and eastern Uttar Pradesh. Individual boats varied, but perhaps the difference Solvyns noted may have been due to the distribution of weight.[1]

Following convention, Solvyns portrays the katrā at sail in the background.

NOTE

1 See Deloche, 2:161.

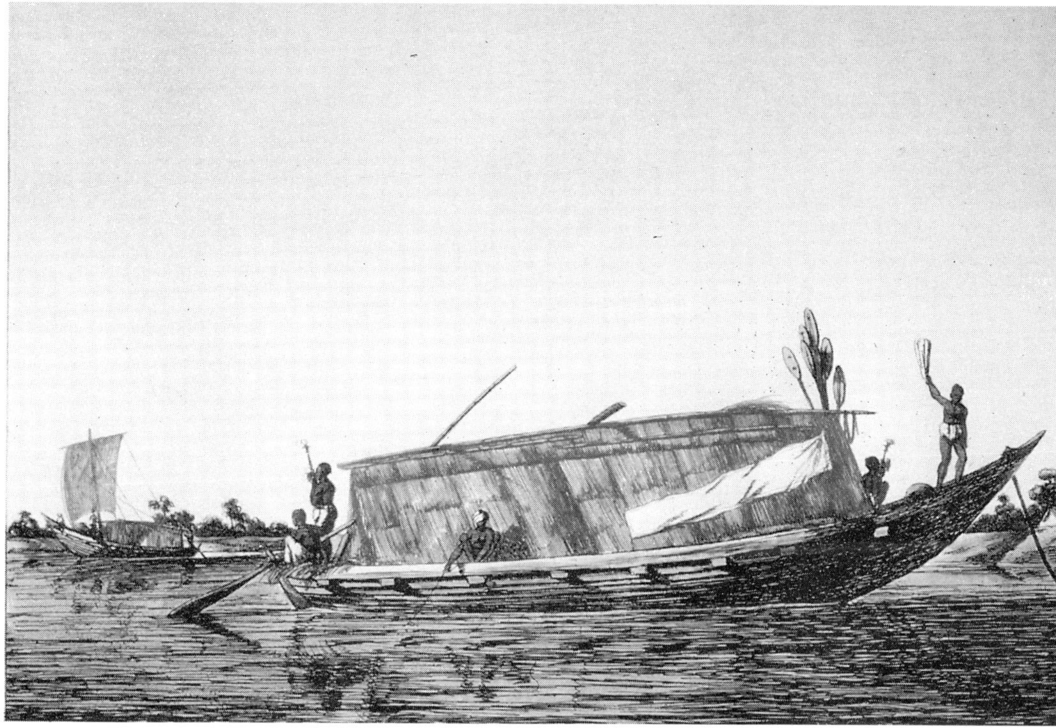

KAṬRĀ. Paris: III.4.5.

24. Bālām

Calcutta: Sec. IX, No. 14. A Chittagong Balaum, built on a Scringee [saraṅgā], having the Planks sown together with Cane or Hemp.
Paris: III.4.6. Balaum.

This is the simplest of all boats and consists meerly of the trunk of a tree hollowed out, to the extremities of which pieces of wood are applied to represent a stern and a prow: the two sides, are boards joined by rottins [rattan] or small bambous without nails: no iron whatsoever enters into their construction: even the anchor is of wood.

The *Balaums* are used in the district of Chittagong: they sometimes come to Calcutta, where they are broken up for the timber. How clumsy soever these boats may be, their construction is superior to that of the northern countries: it is true they are exposed to greater dangers in the arms of the sea which they have to pass, and are built higher in the sides than the river boats, to keep out the waves.

Commentary: Solvyns identifies the bālām—Anglo-Indian "baloon"[1]—with Chittagong, as does *The Anglo-Hindoostanee Hand-Book* in identifying it as a "Mug Boat," referring to the people of Chittagong and Arakan known as Maghs.[2] The *Hand-Book* describes the boat as "having a floor of a single hollowed piece of timber, and raised sides, neatly attached by rattan sewing, with strips of bamboo over the seams."[3]

Bālāms are, in Greenhill's words, "no more than greatly enlarged versions of the simple canoe."[4] In the 1799 *Catalogue*, Solvyns refers to the base of the boat as a "Scringee," *saraṅgā*, the general term for cargo-carrying dugouts, portrayed by Solvyns in Plate 16. This base is hollowed out to leave only thin sides, perhaps no more than one inch in thickness, and on the edges of this keel-like bottom "the sides are raised by means of three and six planks flaring outward and sewn together by means of rattan and coir. Not a single nail is used in these boats," and "the nature of their construction confers upon them a

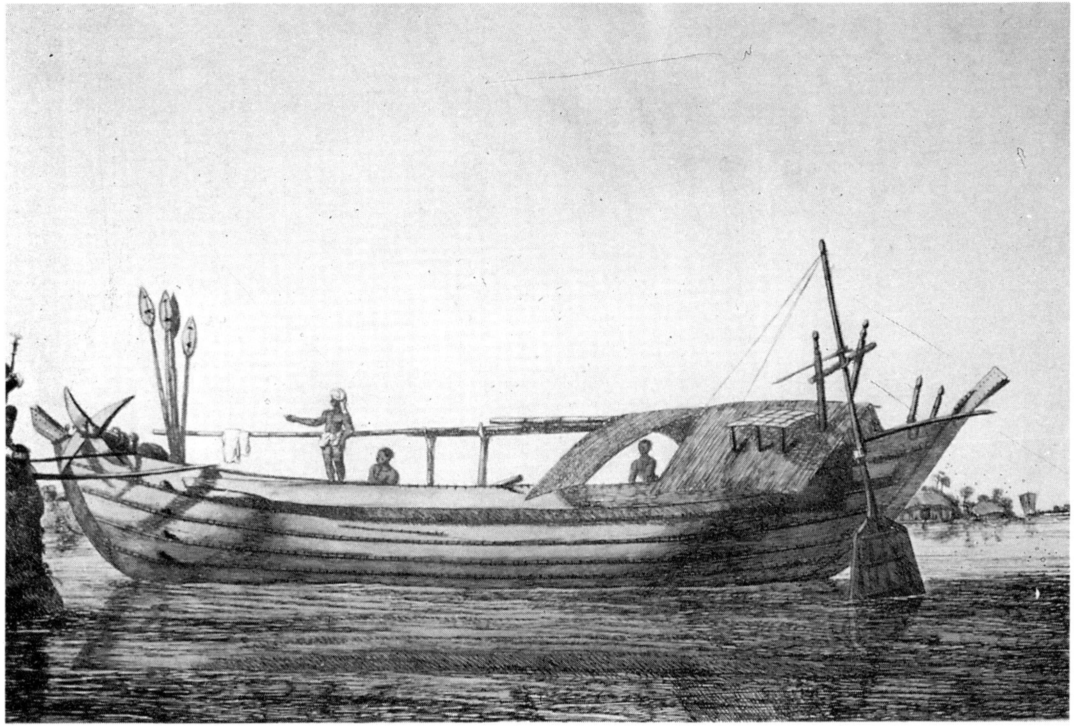

BĀLĀM. Paris: III.4.6.

considerable degree of elasticity and so enables them to bump over a river bar with comparative impunity."[5]

The bow and stern boards, unseen in Solvyns's depiction, are richly decorated in complex designs in vivid color. Greenhill's *Boats and Boatmen of Pakistan,* with extensive discussion of these "powerful" and "impressive" vessels, includes photographs of large sea-going *balams* over 60 feet long, 7 feet deep, and 12 or 14 feet in the beam.[6] These large cargo boats carry crews with up to 30 when rowing. Solvyns does not show the bālām with its mast raised, but although equipped with oars, shown vertically in the print, it is a sailing boat, with the heel of the mast usually stepped (or placed) in a tabernacle made of a heavy log with a deep notch. With stout rigging, the mast carries a squaresail.[7] The anchor depicted aboard the bālām is a wooden grapnel.

Hornell suggests resemblance both in name and construction to boats in South India,[8] and Kerchove, in the *International Maritime Dictionary,* places the *ballam* on the Malabar coast and describes it as a large dugout generally used in hook and line fisheries. He notes that Arabs have copied the design in a planked boat of larger dimensions capable of carrying mast and sail.[9]

NOTES

1 *Hobson-Jobson,* 53.
2 On the Maghs, see Commentatry on Kośā (Pl. 28).
3 Grant and Colebrooke, 115.
4 *Boats and Boatmen of Pakistan,* 114. Also see Deloche, 2:179.
5 Hornell, "The Boats of the Ganges," 194.
6 114-17; photographs, 105. Also see Jansen, *The Country Boats of Bangladesh,* 72-73.
7 Greenhill, *Boats and Boatmen of Pakistan,* 115, and Hornell, "The Boats of the Ganges," 194.
8 "The Boats of the Ganges," 194.
9 33.

25. Gudārā

Calcutta: Sec. VIII, No. 13. A Gudwaree, or Ferry Boat
Paris: III.5.1. Ferry, or Passage on the Ganges.

In different parts, particularly in the neighbourhood of the bazars or markets, there are boats on the Ganges. I have represented one of these, with the company going over, which is composed of women of the lower classes and their children, of *Coulies* or day labourers, Faquirs, Jemidars [*jamidār*],[1] etc. These boats are at times so overloaded, that they get over with the greatest difficulty: they sometimes even sink, and disappear for ever with all the passengers. I have more than once witnessed these accidents; and, what is most remarkable, the Hindoos do not make the slightest effort to save themselves from perishing in the Ganges: they are persuaded that, whatever accident may happen to them in passing that river, proceeds immediately from the express will of God, and that, entire resignation to their fate will ensure them happiness in the next world. Far from lamenting therefore the lot of those who are drowned in this manner, it is a subject of rejoicing to their families, and the memory of it is transmitted with a sort of exaltation to their descendants.

The price of the passage is a meer trifle, either in a boat or a pontoon; but a permission from the Jemidar, or officer of the district, is necessary.

Commentary: In the Calcutta edition, this etching is titled *A Gudwaree*, gudārā, Bengali for ferry boat. The gudārā is again portrayed in the Paris edition (Pl. 34)—though not in the Calcutta collection—with a depiction of ferry boats in passage over rough water.

Here the ferry is loading at the ghāṭ. In mid-river, another gudārā is shown with sail.

NOTE

1 Bengali for the Persian word *zamīndār*, landholder.

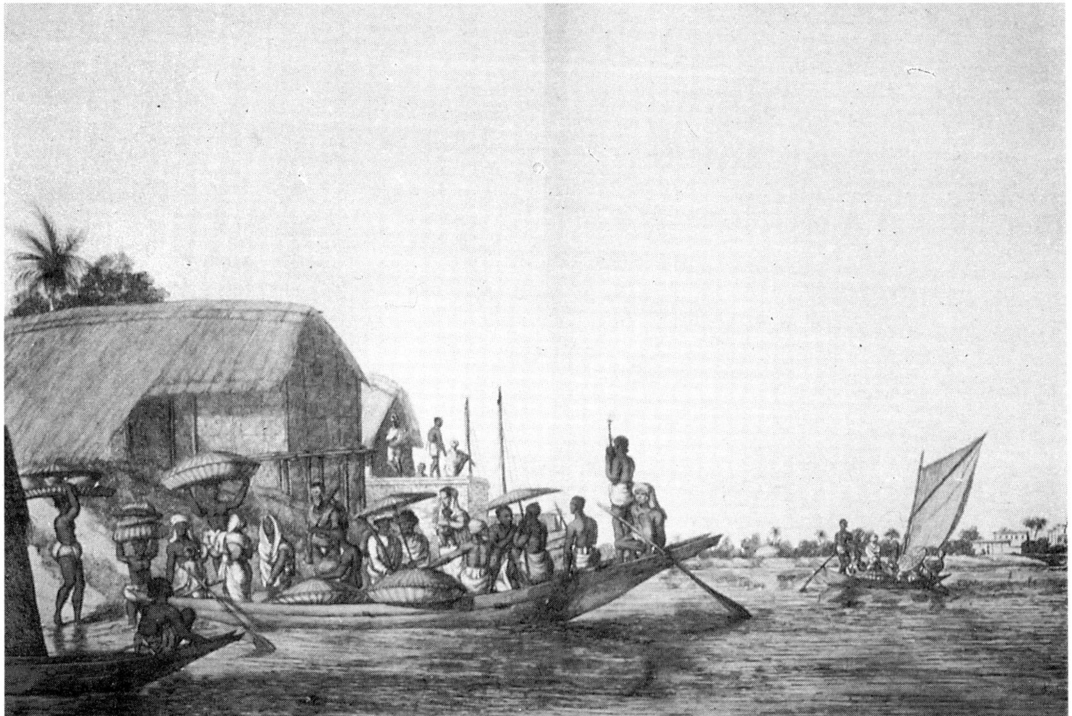

GUDĀRĀ. Paris: III.5.1. (double plate)

26. Brig

Calcutta: Sec. IX, No. 2. A Bengal pariar Brig.
Paris: III.5.2. Brig.

The slightest view of the engraving is sufficient to give an idea of the meanness of this sort of vessel, which is consequently, in all the Indian seas, stigmatized with the appellation of *pariah,* which is given indistinctly, as I have already had occasion to remark in the beginning of the first volume, to all that is bad.

These *Brigs* come from the coast of Coromandel and of Malabar, and bring to Calcutta the produce of those countries. It appears surprising that such indifferent vessels should attempt so long a voyage, till we reflect that they perform it but once in the year, and wait the favourable monsoon to come and return. With this precaution, the Indian seas are without danger for the frailest vessels; but without it, the stoutest ships run great risks. The frigates and company ships, which venture out of the bay of Calcutta in the bad season, frequently put in again dismasted. The passage from Madras to Calcutta requires but five or six days in the good season, and several months in the bad, though the distance between these two towns is but a few degrees.

Commentary: A brig is a two-masted ship and is the smallest seagoing vessel that is square rigged. It is some 90 to 100 feet in length and 24 to 34 feet in breadth, with a burden of 200 to 500 tons.[1] The terms "brig" or "brigantine," however, were often used loosely and were "variously applied by the mariners of different European nations to a peculiar sort of vessel of their own marine."[2] Solvyns depicts a country-made version of this European-style ship and terms it a "pariah," a caste name used to refer to the worst of anything.[3] In his portrayal, as evident in the bow, these are brigs built to handle volume and not for speed.

In his note to the original drawing, Solvyns writes that the "Bengalee Paria (common) Brig" conveys "a pretty correct idea of

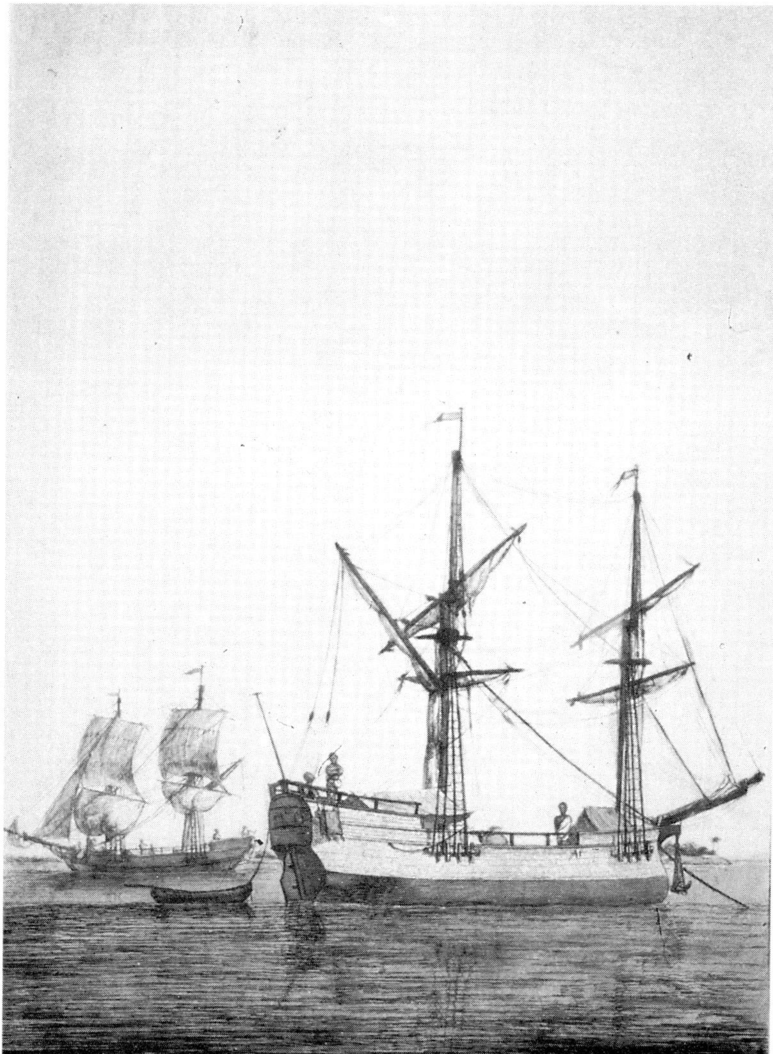

BRIG. Paris: III.5.2.

the naval architecture of the Natives; they are remarkably sparing of iron in building, the chair plates &c are of wood, as also the anchor, or more properly the drag, which is filled with stones." The anchor Solvyns refers to is a cross-armed Indian grapnel, more clearly depicted on the ulāk (Pl. 27).

In the Paris etching, though not in the Calcutta print, a grab (Pl. 20) is portrayed in the background.

NOTES

1 Kerchove, 92.
2 Falconer, *Marine Dictionary* (1787), in Smyth, 134-35.
3 See earlier comment in the introductory "Boats of Bengal," fn. 12, on the use of the term *pariah.*

27. Ulāk

Calcutta: Sec. IX, No. 12. A Wolack,—a large boat for merchandize.
Paris: III.5.3. Wolack.

The *Wolack* resembles the *Bangles* [Pl. 21]. I have represented it on a larger scale, to give a more complete idea of the construction of this boat, and of the different parts which compose it. At a distance is another *Wolack* under sail. The back-ground, as in most of the other prints, is the banks of the river. The *Wolacks* bring rice to Calcutta, where great magazines of it are formed, as well for exportation as for consumption. The covering of the *Wolacks* can be raised or lowered at pleasure. With the wind abaft [toward the stern], they sail tolerably well: but if it blows any way against them, they are very hard to manage, and can not stand the wind and waves. Another inconvenience of the *Wolack* and of many other Hindoo boats, is, that they are so ill calked, that the water easily penetrates them. The insects too are exceedingly troublesome, and, if it were not for the constant smoking, they would be quite insupportable.

Commentary: The ulāk (Anglo-Indian, wollock) is a "bulky baggage boat of Bengal" that Colesworthy Grant likens to the pāṭeli (Pl. 22) in its substantial size. But in contrast to the clink-built pāṭeli, the side planking of the ulāk is laid edge-to-edge and fastened with iron clamps, giving it the appearance of being stitched.[1] With a sharp bow, smooth sides and rounded bottom, the ulāk was generally used to carry grain. Williamson, in his 1810 *East India Vide-Mecum,* wrote that "some of the *woolacks* used by the more opulent native merchants are capable of bearing from fifteen hundred to three thousand *maunds* (eighty to a hundred tons), but their medium may be taken at from four to eight hundred *maunds.*"[2] Prinsep notes that "this boat is the best for tracking and sailing before the wind, and is tolerably manageable with the oar in smooth water."[3]

The enormous rudder—similar to that portrayed on the "Bangles" (Pl. 21) and pāṭeli—"is constructed of a triangular frame on which

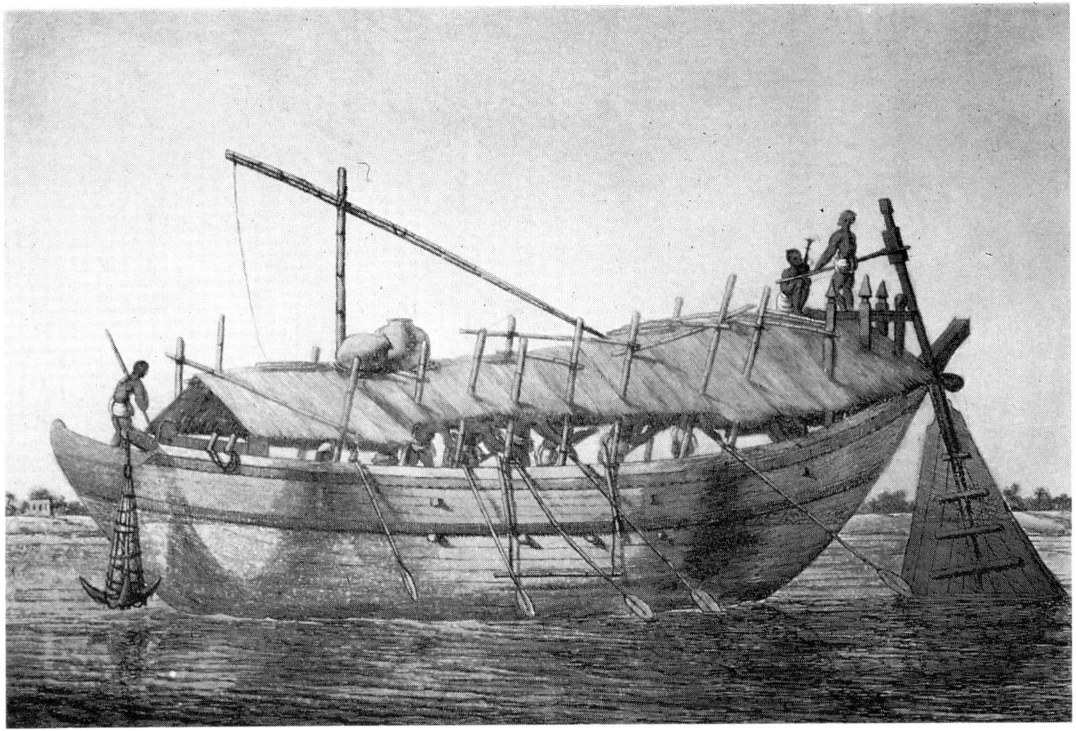

ULĀK. Paris: III.5.3.

are nailed vertical planks strengthened with three or four cross battens."[4]

The etching provides a view of the "cross-armed Indian grapnel anchor," constructed of wood and weighted with stones.[5]

Solvyns slips in the Paris text in referring to another ulāk in the distance. The boat is depicted at sail in the Calcutta etching, but is not shown in the Paris print.

NOTES

1 *Rural Life in Bengal*, 25, with small engraving. On the ulāk, see Deloche, 2:161.

2 383.

3 48. Prinsep illustrates the *oolak* in Appendix A4.

4 Hornell, *Water Transport*, 250.

5 Van Nouhuys, 2-23. Solvyns's etching is reproduced to illustrate the anchor, 22. Solvyns also portrays the grapnel anchor aboard a kośā, Pl. 28.

28. Kośā

Calcutta: Sec. IX, No. 16. A Kose,—peculiar to Chittagong and Luckipore [Lakhipur, on the Brahmputra River in Assam].
Paris: III.5.4. Kose.

This species of boat, much in use in the province of Chittagong, carries sail very well, and can navigate without danger in all the rivers of Hindoostan. The wind has but little power over it, on account of the lowness of its covering. The *Kose* can even stand the sea. Its crew is generally composed of *Mugs*, a dirty and disgusting people, but strong and skilful. They are somewhat of the Malayan race, and will be mentioned hereafter.[1] The *Mugs* are perfectly acquainted with all the passes of the Indian coasts, where the navigation is impeded by a number of small islands. They are frequently obliged to wait for the tide, and can not approach the land without the greatest danger from the tigers, the wild buffaloes, the crocodiles, and other ferocious animals, with which the coasts are infested. The tiger especially are dreaded on account of their audacity: they sometimes even swim to the boats, dart into them with incredible velocity, choose out the plumpest man of the crew, and carry him off to their den. To avoid being surprised by night, the boats are surrounded with netting.

Commentary: The kośā is a small to medium-sized boat of eastern Bengal. They are "more expeditious" than their form promises, Solvyns writes in his note to the original drawing, and they "are said to be strong and safe."

The kośā is flat-bottomed, narrow, and as long as 20 feet. Greenhill describes a "korsha" as "double ended, often without sheer, but some with the flat bottom steeply canted up at eather end, giving the boat a marked sheer. . . ." He writes that he was told that "the name comes from a Bengali word for a small votive vessel used in Hindu temples which is of similar shape to these little boats."[2] The votive vessel is a *kośā*, portrayed by Solvyns in his etching of the Śrotriya Brahmin.[3] Its shape is like the long petal of a plaintain flower, and the boat of the

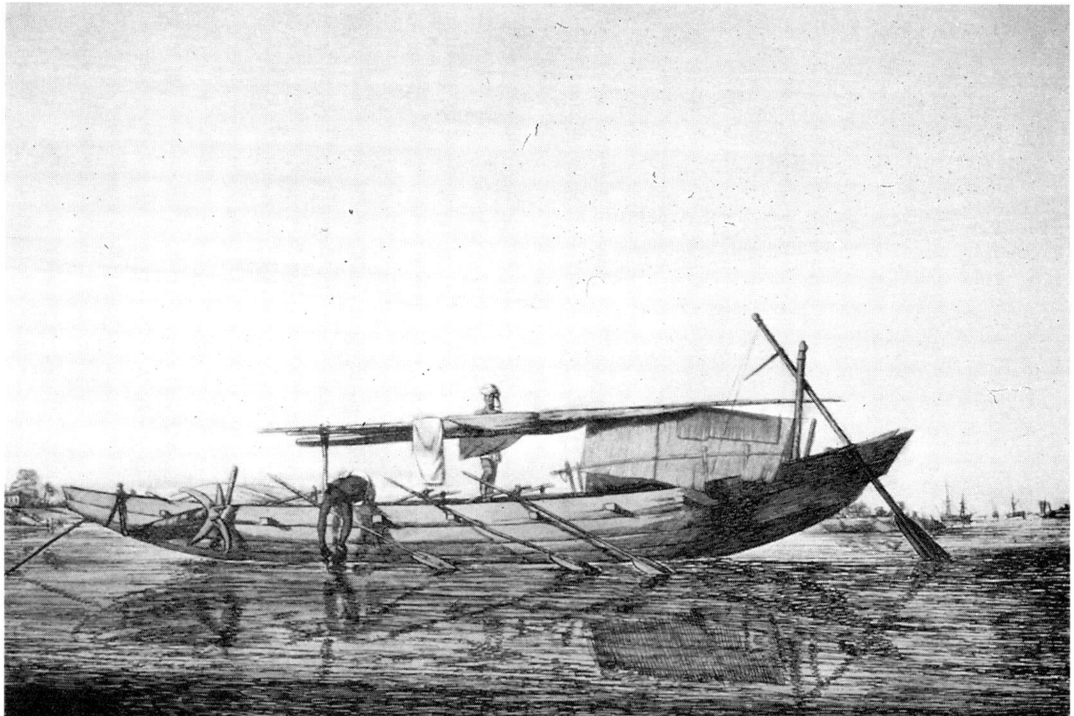

KOŚĀ. Paris: III.5.4.

same name is sometimes described as shaped like a spoon—though that is suggested neither by Solvyns's portrayal nor Greenhill's description.

The kośā, according to Greenhill, is of *chine* construction, with wide planks, fastened by staples, coming up on the sides from the flat bottom.[4] By contrast, Montgomery Martin, in his compilation of survey material on Eastern India by Francis Buchanan, describes the kośā as "clinker-built of Sal."[5] Solvyns makes no reference to clinker construction nor in his depiction does the boat appear to be of that character. Martin writes that "both ends [of the kośā] are nearly the same shape ending in a sharp point, and rise very little above the water. . . . Their bottoms are perfectly flat without any keel [and are] rather unsafe; but, drawing very little water, are exceedingly convenient [in shallow] waters."[6]

Solvyns refers to the *kosa's* capacity to carry sail, but as depicted in the print, the mast is down (with the sail apprently wrapped around it), and it is fitted with three oars on each side.

Kośās are used for fishing and ferrying and, fitted with a thatched covering (*chāuni*), as in Solvyns's portrayal, serve as small cargo carriers.[7] Jansen, in *Country Boats of Bangladesh,* notes that it carries a wide range of goods, but "small size and special shape make it well-suited for the transport of such bulk commodities as stone, bricks, and sand. It is particularly well-suited for small timber hauls."[8] The boat is fitted with a wooden grapnel anchor similar to that shown in Solvyns's portrayal of the ulāk (Pl. 27).

Solvyns identifies the boat with the "Mugs"—*Maghs*—a common name for the Arakanese, ethnically Burman, Buddhist inhabitants of the coast south of Chittagong.[9] They describe themselves by various names, and *Magh* may well be "a foreign epithet, unknown to the Arakanese themselves."[10] The derivation of the name *Magh* is disputed, but from whatever source, the word in Bengali, *mag* or *magh,* as applied to Arakanese raiders, was extended to mean "pirate."[11]

Walter Hamilton, in his 1820 *Description of Hindostan,* writes that "Under the name of Mughs, the Aracaners infested and devastated the lower districts of Bengal, carrying off the inhabitants into slavery."[12] In the seventeenth century, the Portuguese purchased slaves from them for resale. These raids extended well into the eighteenth century, and Rennell's map of 1771 shows wide areas of the Sunderbans—the tiger-infested islands referred to by Solvyns—"depopulated by the Maghs"[13] "So great was the dread of the Mugs" that about 1770 a chain was run across the Hugli river "to protect the port of Calcutta against pirates."[14]

As a result of the Burmese invasions of Arakan in 1782-84, a major portion of the "Mugs" fled north toward Chittagong and into the hills. Although raids continued intermittently, by Solvyns's time, many Arakanese had established peaceful residence in Chittagong, and some ventured to Calcutta, where they soon came to be renowned among Europeans as "the best class of native cooks."[15]

Today in Bangladesh, the Arakanese, generally termed "Marma," are concentrated in the area of Cox's Bazar and, as a distinct group (the Jūmiā Maghs or Khyoungthā, "children of the river"), in the Chittagong Hill Tracks.[16]

NOTES

1 Solvyns includes a Magh in his portrayal *Of the Nations Most Known in Hindoostan*, Paris: III.12.5.
2 *Boats and Boatmen of Pakistan*, 110.
3 Calcutta: Sec. I, No. 1; Paris: I.1.2.
4 *Boats and Boatmen of Pakistan*, 110.
5 4:343.
6 4:343-44.
7 Greenhill, *Boats and Boatmen of Pakistan*, 110.
8 77.
9 Risley, *Tribes and Castes of Bengal*, 2:28-37; *Hobson-Jobson*, 594; O'Malley, *Bengal District Gazetteers: Chittagong*, 60-62; and Rizvi, 60-92, 114-15.
10 Risley, *Tribes and Castes of Bengal*, 2:28-29.
11 Sukumar Sen, 730, gives *mag* as "pirate" and makes no mention of the Arakanese. There is no entry for *magh*. On Magh pirates, see Commentary on Saraṅgā, Pl. 16.
12 *A Geographical, Statistical, and Historical Description of Hindostan and Adjacent Countries*, 1:175.
13 Jamini Mohan Ghosh, *Magh Raiders in Bengal*, 6.
14 Long, *Calcutta in the Olden Times*, 124.
15 *Hobson-Jobson*, 594. Colesworthy Grant, in *An Anglo-Indian Domestic Sketch*, 106, wrote that Mugs are "esteemed by us in the culinary department, being heaven-born cooks from the Burmese quarter."
16 Hunter, *A Statistical Account of Bengal*, 6:39-43, 6:142-43. Hutchinson gives the term Jumiya Magh to the Maghs of the Hill Tracks, and says that they are divided into the "Marama or those who come from Burma, and the Kyongsa or those who live on the river." 29. He discusses Maghs, 28-35.

29. Palwār

Calcutta: Sec. IX, No. 15. A Dacca pulwar,—a commodious and expeditious boat.
Paris: III.5.5. Pulwar.

Of all the Hindoo boats the *Pulwar* is the best built and fittest for inland navigation. In consequence of which the East-India company, it is said, have ordered that no other boat should be employed to transport precious goods, such as silver, muslins, opium, indigo, etc. The *Pulwars* are very light, and carry sail well: of a middle size, and with able rowers, they are sure to pass any other species of boat. Both of its ends are of an equal height; it carries a small mast with a square sail which extends beyond its sides, and sometimes a topsail. The Hindoos call them *Dacca Pulwar*, from the great number which are built in the town of Dacca, where almost all their boats have that form. Since this town, formerly so commercial, has come under the dominion of a Mussulman prince, the *Magies* [*mājhī*, captain] and *Dandys* [*dāṇḍī*, sailor] of the *Pulwars* are Mussulmans, and there are few Hindoos among their crews.

Commentary: The palwār (Anglo-Indian pulwar), "light, manoeuverable and secure,"[1] is a broad, keelless boat, some 60 feet long and capable to carrying 12 to 15 tons.[2] It is the typical cargo river boat of the Dhaka region, "a craft built to carry heavy loads at the lowest possible cost." It is carvel-built, that is, with its hull planks edge to edge rather than overlapping, permitting easy repair. "The single mast is stepped fairly well forward and carries a square sail,"[3] as seen on the boat in the background of Solvyns's portrayal. The palwār Solvyns presents for closer view is anchored and its mast is down.

In his note to the original drawing, Solvyns wrote, "They are remarkable among the Country Boats for safety and expedition," and Europeans generally shared Solvyns's high regard for the palwār. Prinsep described it as "the fastest and most handy boat in use for general traffic."[4]

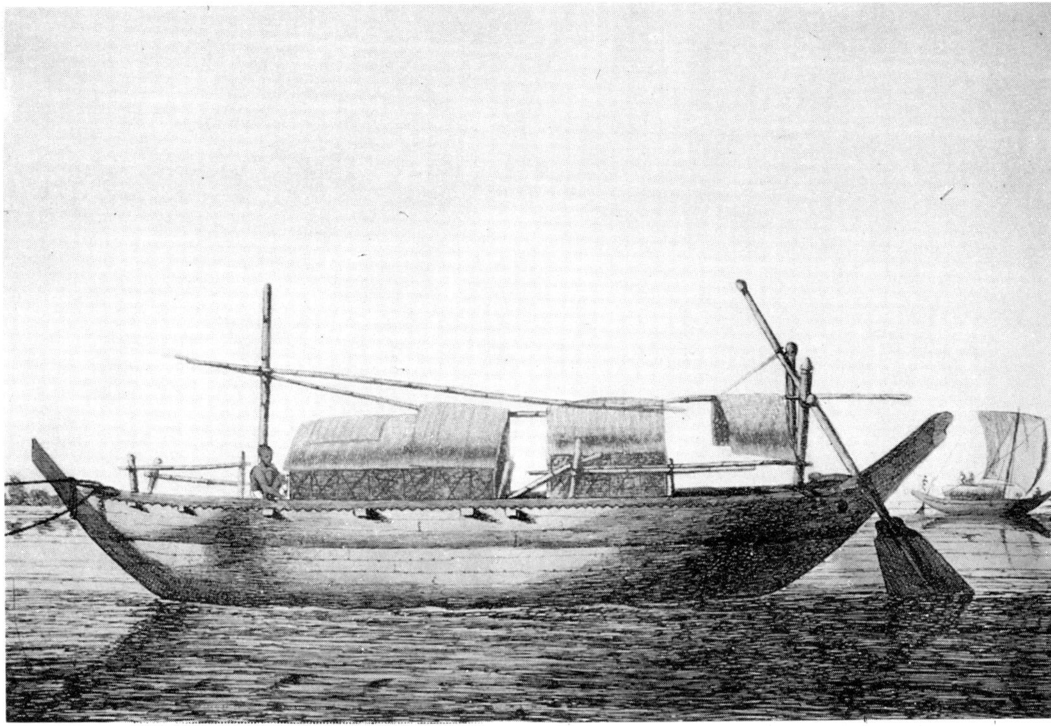

PALWĀR. Paris: III.5.5.

The palwār provides a good example of variable boats with the same name. In eastern Bengal, the Dhaka palwār, as it is known, is "a good, well-constructed barge," but in upper Bengal and Bihar, the name refers to "a small craft sometimes used by a single person" or that was used as a kitchen boat and for accommodation of servants in the flotilla accompanying a bājrā (Pl. 5) or pinnace (Pl. 2) on extended trips. And in parts of Bihar, "palwar" was used for a pilot-boat, of whatever form, that guided others through difficult passages.[5]

NOTES

1 Deloche, 2:162.

2 *Hobson-Jobson*, 737. Greenhill, *Boats and Boatmen of Pakistan*, 85, states that although widely recognized by the name *pulwar*, the accurate word for this "big, beamy, full-ended cargo boat" is *pallar*. Greenhill illustrates various features of the palwār in drawings, 92-96. But, to make any sorting out of the various names more difficult, Jansen, *Sailing Against the Wind*, 70, gives it as *palowary*.

3 Hornell, "The Boats of the Ganges," 190-91.

4 48, illustrated Appendix A4.

5 Deloche, 2:162, fn. 64; Hodges, 39; Colesworthy Grant, *Rural Life in Bengal*, 7, with engraving.

30. Holā

Calcutta: Sec. IX, No. 13. A Hola,—a flat square boat employed to transport Salt from Ingelee [Hijili][1] and Tomlook [Tumluk][2] to Calcutta.
Paris: III.5.6. Hola.

The *Hola* resembles entirely a pontoon, being square at both ends, and very unlike any other boat. It is the only flat-bottomed boat which goes to the mouth of the Ougli [Hugli], where there is so much danger for other boats. It is used to convey to Calcutta, and to a greater distance, the salt of Ingelee, Tomlouck, and its environs. To ship the salt, several *creeks* and *nullahs* [ravines] come out of the little streams, and meet in the river near the sandbanks and shallows, where the salt abounds. These boats are always careful to shelter themselves in some bay at nightfall, or on the appearance of foul weather, and always anchor under the land.

The *Holas* are well masted, and carry good sails, which are in general remarkably white; their cables and anchors too are excellent; notwithstanding all which it still is surprising that they can sail in the Ougli and the Ganges without danger. The *Dandys* [*dāṇḍī*] who are in general of Hindoo origin, live wholly upon rice. Their complexion is darker than that of the other *Dandys*. It is a general remark, that the inhabitants of the mouths of the rivers, where the water is salt, are much blacker than those of the north of Hindoostan, as the inhabitants of Bengal have not so clear a skin as the Hindoos of Behar.

Commentary: The *Anglo-Hindoostanee Hand-Book* describes the holā as having "a circular bow and stern, and great proportionate beam: it is used for heavy freight, such as coals, bricks, *kunkur* [gravel], & c."[3] Solvyns describes the holā as "square at both ends," but, if so, it is surely not evident in his portrayal.

"The *hola*," Hornell writes, "is the humble coal and brick carrier, dirtiest and most unkempt of Hoogly craft. Built on the same lines as the larger bhar [bhur, Pl. 33], its mast is usually a single pole placed rather further forward and carries only a single squaresail. The

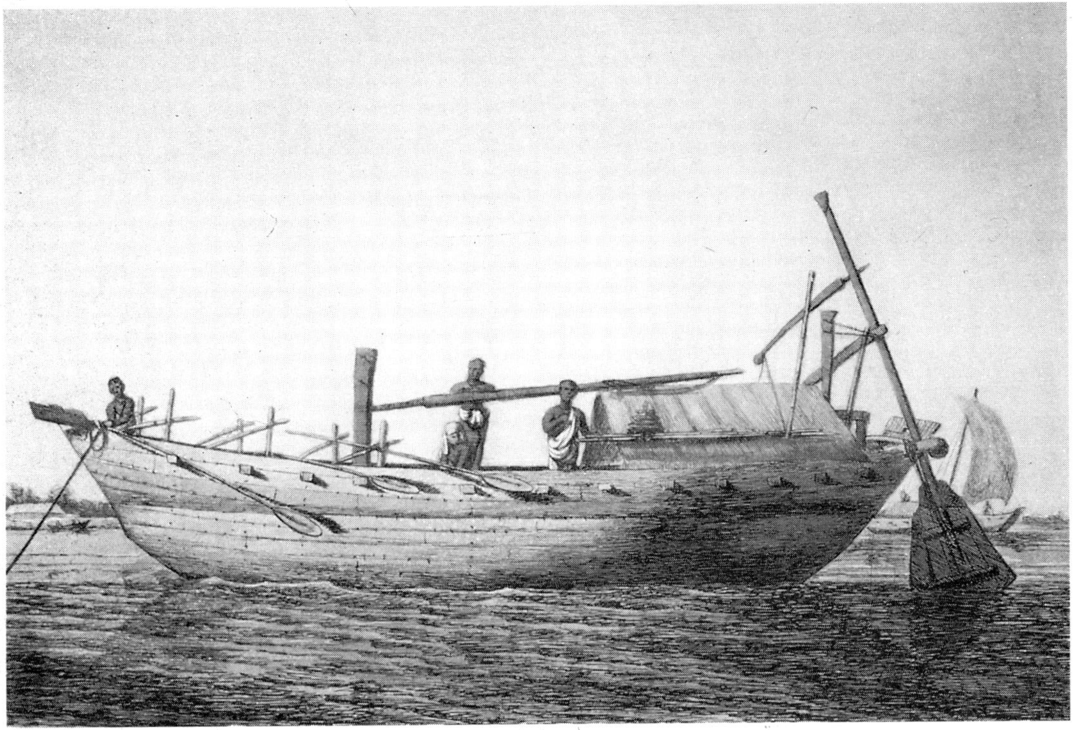

HOLĀ. Paris: III.5.6.

rudder is of the sweep type, suspended from the quarter and worked by the steersman from the usual little bamboo platform. . . . When the *hola* is loaded, the crew of four or six men pull their long paddles, sitting at the fore end; when it is light, they pull standing."[4]

NOTES

1 Also Hidgelee, Ingellie, etc., a town at the mouth of the Hugli. See Deloche, 2:162-64.

2 Corrupted as Tumlook and Tomberlee, Tumluk is an ancient port on the west side of the Hugli near its mouth.

3 Henry Grant and Colebrooke, 115.

4 *Water Transport,* 251, figure 252. Also see Hornell, "The Boats of the Ganges," 194.

31. Sloop

Calcutta: Sec. IX, No. 3. A Sloop, employed for the Coast trade, and to carry down the River the Cargo for large ships.
Paris: III.6.2. Sloop.

The *Sloops* are used to carry goods to and from the merchant-ships which are laded or unladed. They are employed particularly at Cutgerie, at Engelee, at Diamonds harbour, and near Culpee. The East-India company have many in its service. They have five or six men on board, who are well acquainted with all the dangers of the river. They carry masts and sails, are strong and well built, but not swift sailors. With an European crew, they could stand the open sea. Some of them now have cordage and anchors, like European vessels. The print gives a sufficient idea of their form.

Commentary: The sloop is a small European style vessel with one mast, fore-and-aft rigged (and often, as in Solvyns's portrayal, a square topsail), a short standing bowsprit, and a jib set on a stay. Kerchove states that they usually have one headsail, the foresail and jib forming one sail.[1] In his note to the original drawing of the sloop, Solvyns writes that "altho from their appearance they may be considered unsafe, from a proper attention to the season for sailing, few accidents happen."

In a signed watercolor drawing of the sloop, from the album assembled by Solvyns's widow, Solvyns notes the length as 60 feet and breadth as 18 feet.[2] The sloop is included in a waterfront scene that one of Solvyns's Indian assistants produced as a composite of Solvyns's individual portrayals.[3]

Solvyns describes the sloop as used where Indiamen, unable to proceed further upriver, found safe anchorage. In the days of sail, accounts of travel to Bengal[4] almost always make reference to these anchorages, for here, passengers and goods were tranferred to smaller ships, like the sloop or pinnace (Pl. 2), for transport upriver to Calcutta. Diamond Harbor, 41 miles below Calcutta on the east

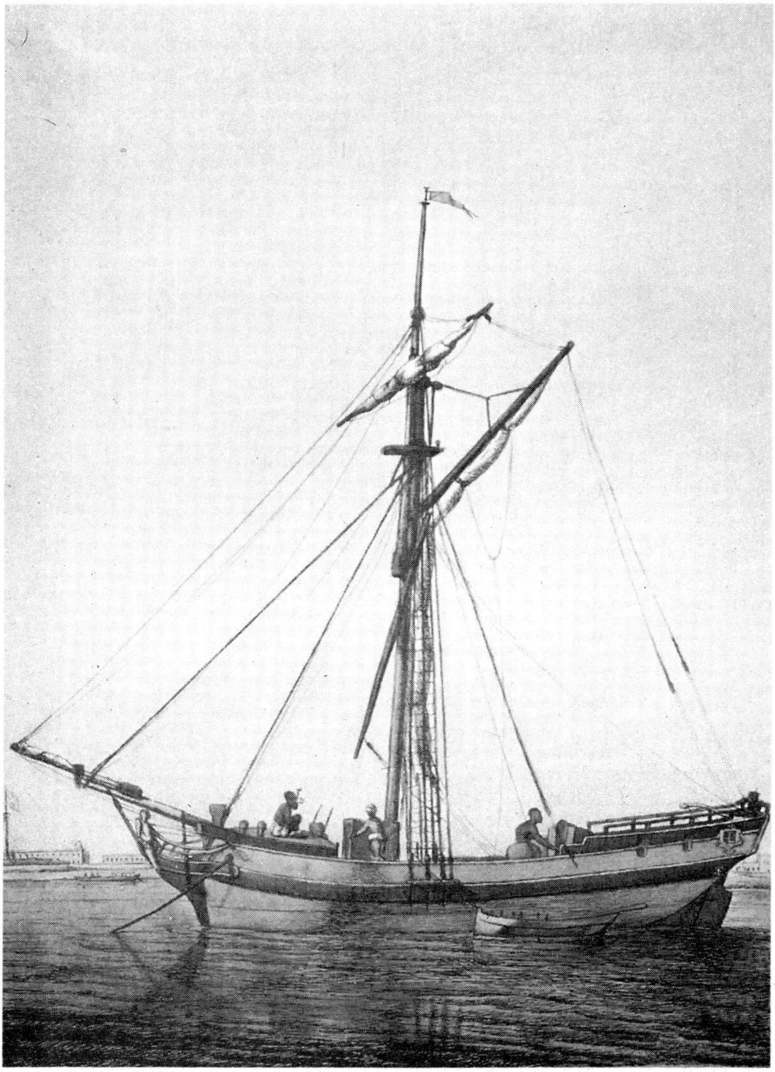

SLOOP. Paris: III.6.2.

bank of the Hugli, was the highest point that could be reached by the larger Indiamen. The village itself was on the edge of swamps and was regarded as "exceedingly unhealthy."[5] Kulpi (Culpee, Coulpy), just below Diamond Harbor, also provided good anchorage, but was less favored.

Kijari (Cutgerie or Kedgeree), at the mouth of the Hugli, provided a healthier situation than Diamond Harbor and was a usual anchorage for larger Indiamen.[6] Walter Hamilton advised that that "ships of war, unless compelled by strong reasons, should never go higher up the river. . . ."[7] Indiamen also anchored at Hijili (Engelee, Ingelee, or Hidgelee), on west side of the Hugli esturary, as well as Balasore and Sagar Island.

NOTES

1 688.

2 The album, discussed in Hardgrave, *A Portrait of the Hindus* (forthcoming), contained 41 drawings and watercolors. Solvyns's widow, Marie Anne, presented the album to friend of the artist in 1829, and in the mid-1980s, it came onto the market. It was subsequently broken for the sale of individual drawings. The drawing, "A Sloop," c. 1795, is now in the collection of the Indian Office Library (WD 4124) and is reproduced in India Office Library and Records, *Annual Report, 1985-1986,* 27, with details about the acquisition, 31; in Losty, "The Belgian Artist F.B. Solvyns," 8; in Kattenborn, 3:294, Pl. 48.

3 The drawing, 42.6 x 60.3 cm, is in the India Office Library, Add Or 4307, and is reproduced in Losty, "The Belgian Artist F.B. Solvyns," 7. Losty dates the drawing about 1800.

4 See, for example, the entries in Nair, *Calcutta in 19th Century.*

5 Walter Hamilton, *A Geographical, Statistical, and Historical Description of Hindostan and Adjacent Countries,* 1:141. Also see his *East India Gazetteer,* 1:510, and Heber, 1:11; Long, *Calcutta in the Olden Time,*10-11; *Hobson-Jobson,* 317.

6 *Hobson-Jobson,* 477.

7 *A Geographical, Statistical, and HistoricalDescription of Hindostan and Adjacent Countries,* 1:141, and *East India Gazetteer,* 2:80.

32. Towboat

Calcutta: Sec. VIII, No. 11. A Tow Boat, to assist ships, &c. in the dangerous navigation of the Houghly River.
Paris: III. 6.3. Towboat.

These are boats which help the ships coming from sea to enter the Ganges and the Ougly, and are of very great service in this navigation, which is full of difficulties. They are of a pointed form, with their broadest surface above the water; and so light that the least motion makes them incline from side to side. They carry eight or ten sailors, generally boys, with small oars, except the *Magie* [*mājhī*, captain]. They spend their lives aboard their boats, and sleep under the sails. They are ill fed and ill paid, and are satisfied with a little rice and tobacco. Their constant living on the water, and drinking frequently brackish water, gives their skin a deeper tint than that of the other *Dandys* [*dāṇḍī*, sailor].

Commentary: Solvyns does not here use the Bengali word for towboat, and in the French text for the Paris edition, he uses the term *chaloupe de remorque.* A *chaloupe*—shallop in English—is a different category of boat and is usually an open boat with no deck, powered by oars and/or a single mast.

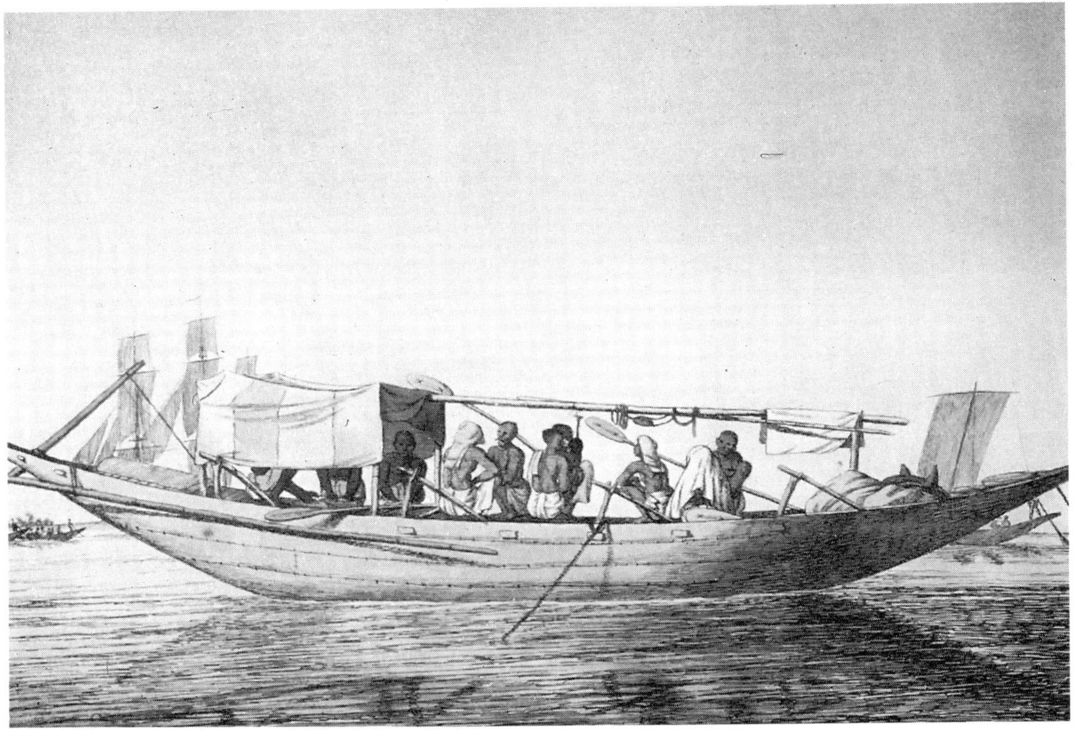

TOWBOAT. Paris: III.6.3.

33. Bhur

Calcutta: Sec. IX, No. 6. A Burr,—used for the inland rice trade and to load and unload ships.
Paris: III.6.4. Burr.

The *Burr* is an open boat, with three or four men, used to lade and unlade the ships in the road. There are a certain number of them at Calcutta; their crews are generally composed of the refuse of the *Dandys* [*dāṇḍī*, sailor]. The *Burrs* are often without cordage, anchors, or oars; and yet their construction is well enough adapted to the service for which they are intended. Like the rest of the Calcutta boats, the *Burr* is lower before than behind, in order probably to stand the swell at high tides. When the phenomenon whose dreadful effects I have already described [North-Wester, Pl. 1] takes place, all the vessels which have not been able to take shelter in time, take care to present their poop to the wave.

Commentary: The bhur (also bharā) is a cargo river boat,[1] the name derived from the Bengali word *bharā*, meaning cargo or load.[2] *Hobson-Jobson* gives the Anglo-Indian word as *bora*.[3] The seventeenth century traveler Thomas Bowrey wrote that "The boora . . . being a very floaty light boat, rowinge with 20 to 30 Owars, these carry Salt peeter and Other Goods (from Hugly) downewards, and some trade to Dacca with Salt; they also Serve for tow boats for the Ships bound up or downe the River."[4]

The bhur has an open hold and a small matted shelter astern for the crew.[5]

Stavorinus, in his *Voyages to the East-Indies*, 1768-71, provides a detailed description of a boat that his translator identifies as a "bur" of Bengal: "The vessels which are used for inland navigation, on the *Ganges*, are very lightly built of thin deals, without either keel or side-timbers. The edges of the planks are fastened together with staples, and the seams are stopped up with moss, and payed with grease. The largest width of them is about one-third of their whole length. . . ; they

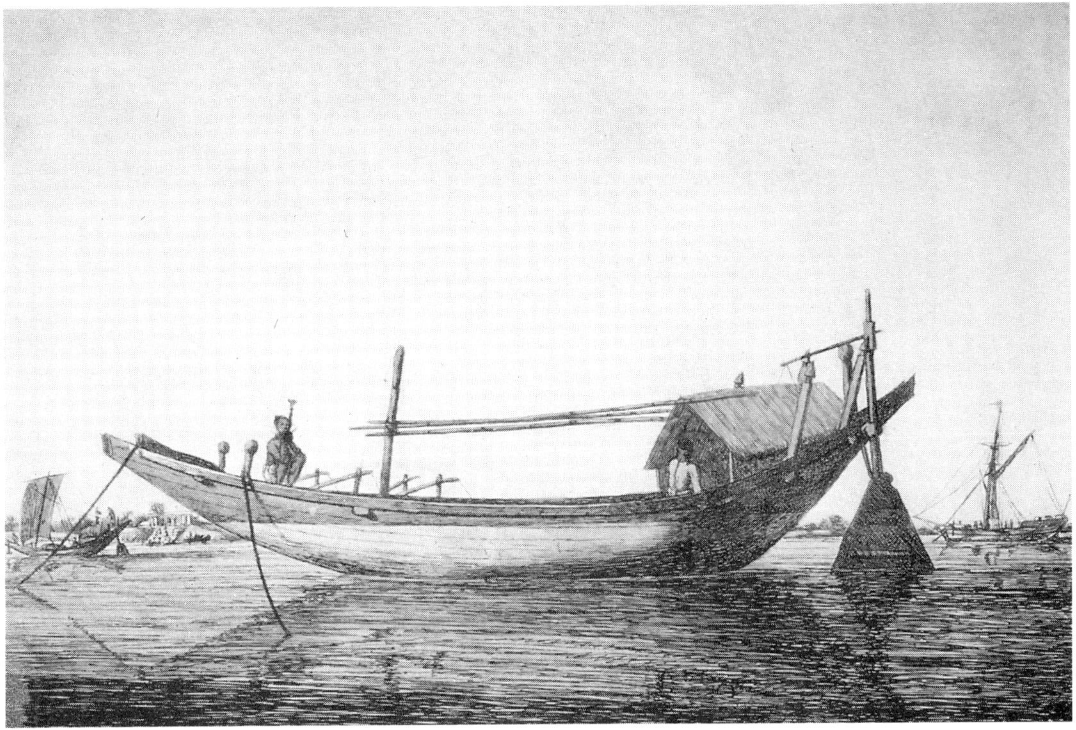

BHUR. Paris: III.6.4.

are very sharp forwards, and are not very high above the water. Although they are of different sizes, they are all the same shape and construction; and some of them can load fifty thousand pounds of weight of merchandize, and more."[6]

The translator's note, in identifying the boat as a bhur, quotes (without attribution) the artist William Hodges's description: Bhurs, Hodges writes in his *Travels*, "are large rude barks, the sides of which are raised very high, and sewed together with the fibres of the cocoanut tree. They have only a single mast, with a large square sail, and the bottoms of them are nearly flat. They take in a great quantity of water from their sides and bottoms, which compels the crew to employ some people continually in bailing. They are used for the farrying of cotton, and other very bulky materials, the weight of which cannot bear any proportion to their size."[7]

Hornell describes the bhur as the principal jute carrier of Bengal. "Of great beam, with low bows, bluff and rounded, and a stern but slightly eleveated, it is undecked except for a short distance aft, where a thatched cabin is erected; behind this, right at the stern, is a small raised platform nearly level with the cabin roof, for the accommodation of the helmsman."

"The cargo is packed in the open waist, and rises high above the gunwales, kept in place by a temporary loose framework of bamboos on each side and protected from the weather by tarpaulins, or mats.

"The mast, made up of two lengths spliced roughly together, is stepped amidships. A huge squaresail, often much tattered, carries this clumsy vessel along at a fair speed when favoured with a good wind. A topsail is added whenever possible. Without a good wind progress is slow. . . . When there is need to row, the men work long sweeps from on top of the cargo. Against the stream these boats have to tracked laboriously along the bank by the crew."[8]

NOTES

1 Sukumar Sen, 720.
2 Ibid., 702.
3 *Hobson-Jobson*, 105. Also see Deloche, 2:162, fn.66.
4 229.
5 Henry Grant and Colebrooke, 115.
6 1:465.
7 38.
8 *Water Transport*, 251. Also see "The Boats of the Ganges," 193-94.

34. Gudārā

Calcutta: Sec. VIII, No. 13. A Gudwaree, or Ferry Boat.
Paris: III.6.5. Gudwaree.

In the preceding number [Pl. 25] I spoke in general terms of the *Ferries* on the river; I shall now say a few words of the boats which are employed. They are called *Gudwarees* in the Hindoo language, and are of the same species as all the others. The boatmen are so skilful, that, though there may be a great swell in the river, and that they carry but one small sail, they make their passage very expeditiously, with a considerable number of passengers. No European boat, however well built, can be better managed than the *Gudwarees.* Nevertheless Europeans are frequently afraid of passing in these ferryboats, and prefer a *Pansway* [pānsi, Pl. 9] or a *Dingee* [ḍiṅgi, Pl. 11]. Only those of an inferior class use the *Gudwarees.*

Commentary: The Bengali for ferry is *gudārā* or *kheyā.* Here gudārās are depicted in crossing what is probably the Hugli in rough water. The etching is not included in the Calcutta edition.

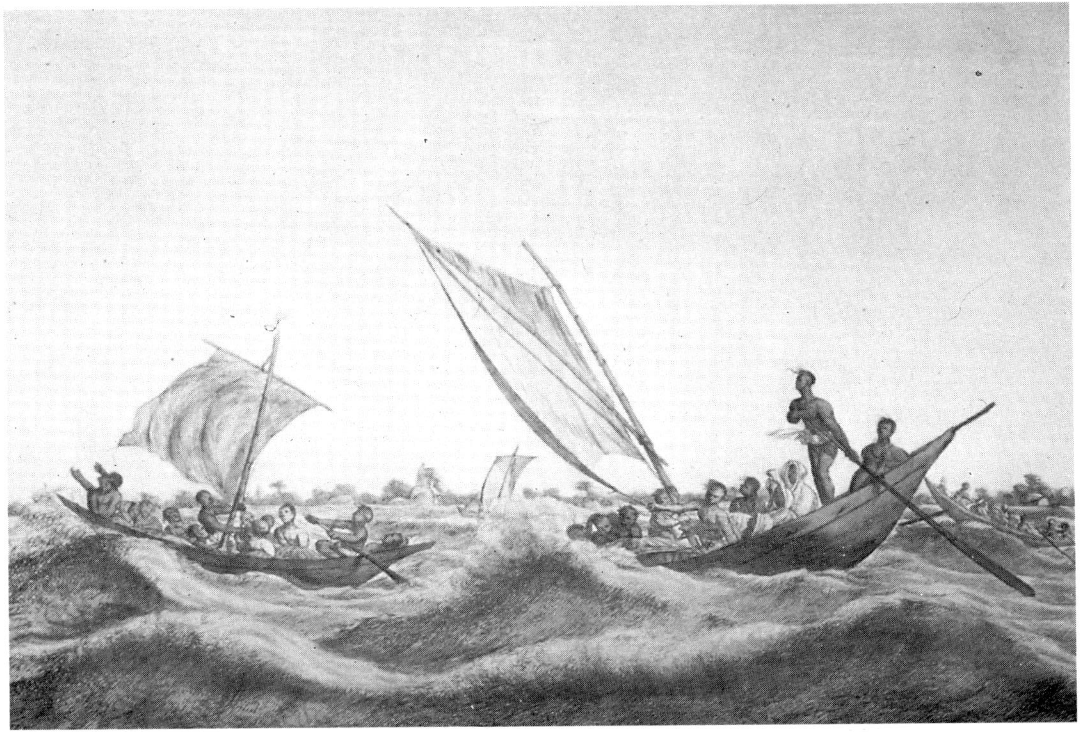

GUDĀRĀ. Paris: III.6.4.

35. Iṭā Ḍiṅgi

Calcutta: Sec. IX, No. 17. A Yet-Dingee,—boat for carrying bricks.
Paris: III.6.6. Yet Dingee.

Here we have another species of boat, called a *Dingee,* and used for carrying bricks: the print represents this boat on shore, a situation which I chose purposely to give an idea of the construction of the Hindoo boats in general. In the building of a boat the Hindoos begin by choosing a large piece of timber, which they bend as they please. To the two ends of this they attach another piece thicker than it, and cover this simple frame with planks: but they have a particular manner of joining these planks to each other, by flat cramps with two points, which enter the boards to be joined, and use common nails only to join the planks to the knee. For the sides of the boat they have pieces of wood, which outpass the planks. This method is as solid as it is simple: and the mode of uniting the planks is not unworthy of the imitation of Europeans.

Commentary: Solvyns's *yet* is *iṭā,* meaning "brick," and ḍiṅgi (Pl. 11) is a small boat. The scene depicts the boat being loaded with bricks at the site of a kiln.

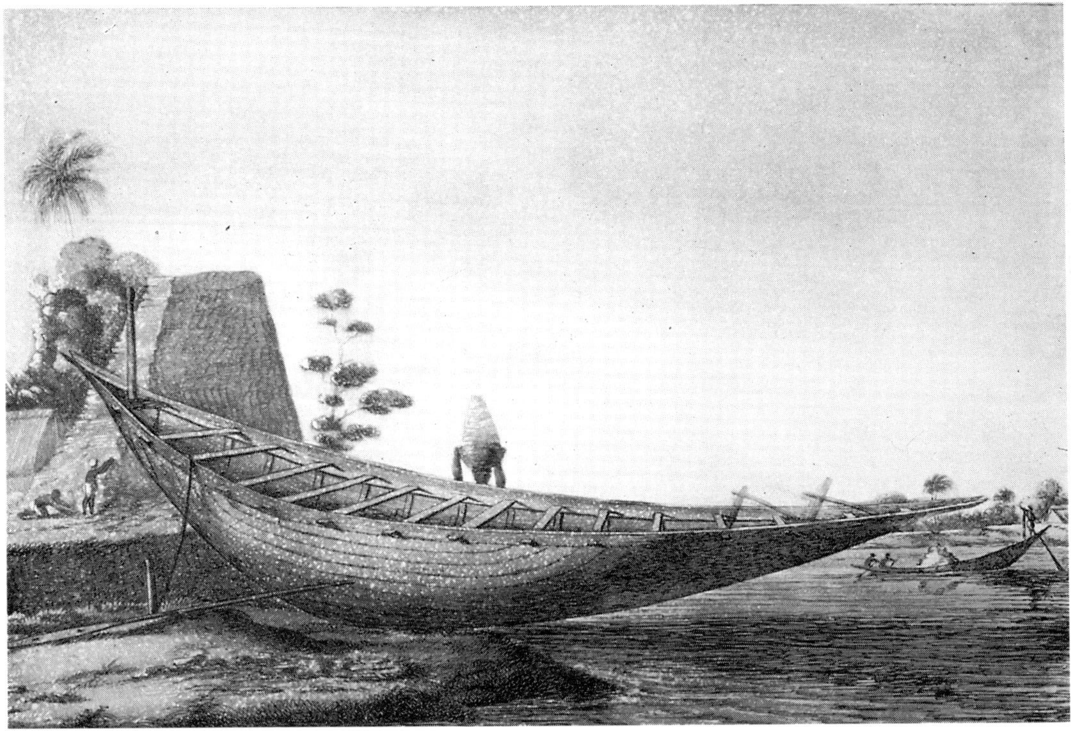

IṬĀ ḌIṄGI. Paris: III.6.5.

36. Vessels of All Sorts

Paris: III.12.6. Vessels of All Sorts.

Six numbers of this volume have been employed for the navigation of the Hindoos; but it did not enter into my plan, to describe the private boats, nor the foreign Indian vessels. I have endeavoured to unite in this print every object of this kind. Here are the high vessels of the Red Sea and Persian gulph, the Grabs [Pl. 20], the ships of the Maldive isles, made of bambous and coconut trees, masts cordage and anchors. The boats employed in the pearl fishery on the coast of Ceylan, the Vliegers of Batavia, the Proues of Malacca, remarked for their swiftness: the Catamarans of Madras, and infine the Chinese Jonques. Among all this imperfect shipping though well adapted to the seas and climates they frequent, I have placed an European frigate, and a boat, as a sufficient proof of the superiority of our naval architecture over that of the Indian nations, and particularly the Hindoos.

Commentary: In Solvyns's composite depiction, on the far right, split by the frame, is the Chinese junk, with its distinctive sail. Just to the left of it, is the frigate, in broadside—portrayed, marine painting specialist Daniel Finamore indicates, as it would look in a treatise on naval architecture, with every sail that she carries set. She would never have looked like this at sea, especially near shore. Solvyns does use the term "frigate" correctly, Finamore notes, showing a full-rigged three masted ship, with a single gun deck. The ship to the far left, stern view, is of seventeenth century design, and Solvyns almost surely copied the image from a painting rather than from drawings he may have made while in India.[1]

Other boats are not clearly distinguished, but Solvyns refers to various vessels that might be encountered, including a catamaran of Madras, though it is nowhere evident in the etching. The catamaran a raft of logs (usually three) lashed together, navagated typically by two men. The Tamil word is *kattumaram*, literally *kaṭṭu* (to tie) +

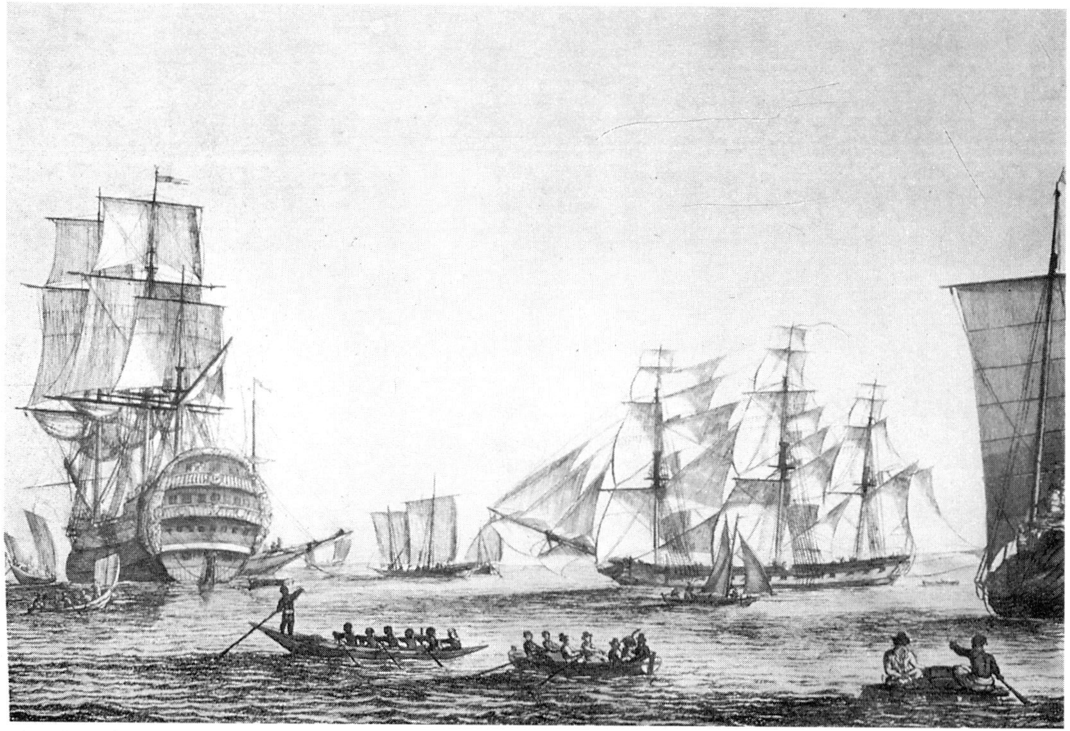

VESSELS OF ALL SORTS. Paris: III.12.6. (double plate)

maram (tree or log). Solvyns distinguishes the boats used in the pearl fisheries off Ceylon, but these were usually kaṭṭumaram.[2]

The "proue" of Malacca is the Malay *prāū*, a particular kind of galley used in the Straits and referred to by Solvyns in his portrayal of Penang (Pl. 13).

Solvyns's reference to Vliegers of Batavia is mystifying. There was a Dutch marine artist named Simon Jocobsz de Vlieger (c. 1600-1653), but no identifiable type of boat by that name. Five Dutch vessels bore the name of the artist, but this hardly seems what Solvyns's intends to convey.[3]

NOTES

1 I am grateful to Daniel Finamore, Curator, Peabody Essex Museum, Salem, Massachusetts, for his help in identifying the ships depicted in the etching.

2 See Deloche, 2:179-81; Edye, 4; Hornell, *Water Transport*, 61-67; and Hornell, "The Origins and Ethnological Significance of Indian Boat Designs," 169-72.

3 Although no boats styled "Vliegers" can be found, the Nederlands Scheepvaartmuseum, Amsterdam, lists five vessels named "Vlieger," one of which was an East Indiaman of 1669. None would fit Solvyns's description. Personal communication, January 6, 1998.

Bibliography

Admiral Paris' Native Boats of Asia and the Pacific, 1841: The catalog of an exhibition and sale of hand-coloured original lihtographs of native craft of Asia and the Pacific executed in 1841 by François-Edmond Paris in his Essai sur la construction navale des peuples extra-Europeeens. Singapore: Antiques of the Orient, 1989.

Archer, Mildred. "Baltazard Solvyns and the Indian Picturesque." *The Connoisseur* 170 (January 1969): 12-18.

———. and W.G. Archer. "Francois Baltazard Solvyns: Early Painter of Calcutta Life." In *Science, Philosophy and Culture: Essays Presented in Honour of Humayun Kabir's Sixty-Second Birthday,* edited by Frank Moraes et al., 1-10. Bombay: Asia Publishing House, 1968.

Archibald, E.H.H. *Dictionary of Sea Painters.* Woodbridge, Suffolk: Antique Collector's Club, 1980.

Berko, Patrick, and Vivian Berko, eds. *Marines van Belgische schilders geboren tussen 1750 en 1875* [Marine Paintings by Belgian Artists Born Between 1750 and 1875], Tr. of 1981 French edition. Brussels: Editions Laconti, 1984.

Bernstein, Henry T. *Steamboats on the Ganges.* Bombay: Orient Longmans, 1960.

Bowrey, Thomas. *A Geographical Account of Countries Round the Bay of Bengal, 1669 to 1679.* Edited by Sir Richard Carnac Temple. 2nd series, No. 12. Cambridge; Hakluyt Society, 1905.

Bulley, Anne. *The Bombay Country Ships* [1790-1833]. London: Curzon Press, 2000.

Busteed, H.E., *Echoes from Old Calcutta.* 3rd ed. Calcutta: Thacker, Spink, 1897.

Crooke, William. *Things India, being notes on various subjects.* London: John Murray, 1906. Reprinted, New Delhi: Oriental Books Reprint Corporation, 1972.

Daniel, J.C. *The Book of Indian Reptiles.* Bombay: Bombay Natural History Society, 1983.

Das Gupta, Tamonash C. *Aspects of Bengali Society from Old Bengali Literature.* Calcutta: Univesity of Calcutta, 1935.

Deb, Raja Binaya Krishna. *The Early History and Growth of Calcutta.* Edited by Subir Ray Choudhuri. Calcutta: Riddhi, 1977 [1905].

Dewar, Douglas. *In the Days of the Company.* Calcutta: Thacker, Spink & Co., 1920.

Dictionary of National Biography. Edited by Leslie Stephen and Sidney Lee. Oxford: Oxford University Press, 1921-1922.

Edye, John. "Description of the Various Classes of Vessels Constructed and Employed by the Natives of the Coasts of Coromandel." *Journal of the Royal Asiatic Society of Great Britain and Ireland* 1 (1834): 1-14.

Fennis, Jan. *Trésor du langage des Galères.* 3 vols. Tübingen: Niemeyer, 1995.

Fenton, Mrs. E. *Journal of Mrs. Fenton—A Narrative of her life in India, the Isle of France (Mauritius), and Tasmania During the years 1826-1830.* Edited by H.W. Lawrence. London: Edward Arnold, 1901.

Ghosh, Jamini Mohan. *Magh Raiders in Bengal.* Calcutta: Bookland, 1960.

Ghosh, Suresh Chandra. *The Social Condition of the British Community in Bengal 1857- 1800.* Leiden: Brill, 1970.

Gilchrist, J.B. *The General East India Guide and Vade Mecum [Being a Digest of the work of the late Capt. Williamson].* London: Kingsbury, Parbury, & Allen, 1815.

Grandpré, L. De. *A Voyage in the Indian Ocean and to Bengal, Undertaken in the Year 1789 and 1790.* London: G. & J. Robinson, 1803.

Grant, Colesworthy. *Rural Life in Bengal.* Calcutta: Stamp Digest, 1984 [1866].

Grant, Henry, and Edward Colebrooke. *The Anglo-Hindoostanee Hand-Book; or Stranger's Self-Interpreter and Guide to Colloquial and General Intercourse with the Natives of India.* Calcutta: W. Thacker; London: Smith, Elder & Co., 1850.

Greenhill, Basil. *Boats and Boatmen of Pakistan.* Newton Abbot, Devon: David & Charles, 1971.

———. "River Boats of Bangladesh." *Classic Boat* 54 (December 1992): 14-19.

Grierson, George A. *Bihar Peasant Life, Being a Discursive Catalogue of the Surroundings of the People of that Province.* Delhi: Cosmo, 1975 [1885].

Hamilton, Walter. *East India Gazetteer,* 2nd ed., 2 vols. London: Parbury, Allen & Co., 1828.

———. *A Geographical, Statistical, and Historical Description of Hindostan and Adjacent Countries.* 2 vols. Delhi: Oriental Publishers, 1971 [1820].

Hardgrave, Robert L., Jr. "A Portrait of Black Town: Baltazard Solvyns in Calcutta, 1791-1804." In *Changing Visions, Lasting Images: Calcutta Through 300 Years,* edited by Pratapaditya Pal, 31-46. Bombay: Marg, 1990.

———. *A Portrait of the Hindus: Balthazar Solvyns Life and Work.* Forthcoming

———, and Stephen M. Slawek. *Musical Instruments of North India: Eighteenth Century Portraits by Baltazard Solvyns.* New Delhi: Manohar, 1997.

Hastings, Marquess of [Frances Rawdon-Hastings]. *The Private Journal of the Marquess of Hastings* [1813-18]. Edited by his daughter. 2 vols. London: Saunders and Otley, 1858.

Heber, Reginald. *Narrative of a Journey Through the Upper Provinces of India, From Calcutta to Bombay, 1824-1825.* 2d ed. 3 vols. London: John Murray, 1828.

Hedges, William [1681-1687]. *Diary of Hedges.* Notes by Henry Yule. 3 vols. London: Hakluyt Society, 1887-1889.

Hickey, William [1749-1809]. *Memoirs.* Edited by Alfred Spencer. 4 vols. New York: Knopf, 1913-1925.

Hobson-Jobson: A Glossary of Colloquial Anglo-Indian Words and Phrases. By Henry Yule and A.C. Burnell. 2nd ed., edited by William Crooke. Sittingbourne, Kent: Linguasia, 1994 [1886, 1903].

Hodges, William. *Travels in India, during the years 1780, 1781, 1782 & 1783.* London: J. Edwards, 1793.

Hornell, James. "The Boats of the Ganges," *Memoirs of the Asiatic Society of Bengal* (1924), 8: 171-238.

———. "The Origins and Ethnological Significance of Indian Boat Designs," *Memoirs of the Asiatic Society of Bengal* (1920), 7:139-256.

———. *Water Transport: Origins and Evolution.* Cambridge: Cambridge University Press, 1946.

Hostyn, Norbert. "De Zee en de Kunst: Frans-Balthasar Solvijns" [The Sea and Art]. *Neptunus* (Ostend), July 1980, 46-47.

———. "Frans-Balthasar Solvyns." *Het Visserijblad* (Ostend), August 6, 1982, 19-20.

———. "Omtrent een Gezicht op de Haven van de Stad Oostende" [About a View of the Harbor of the City of Ostend]. *Bulletin des Musées Royaux d'Art d'History* (Brussels), 1984, 114-18.

———. "Schilders van de zee," *Openbaar Kunstbezit in Vlaanderen* 1 (1984), n.p.

———. "Solvyns, François-Balthazar." In *Marines van Belgische schilders geboren tussen 1750 en 1875* [Marine Paintings by Belgian Artists Born Between 1750 and 1875], edited by Patrick Berko and Vivian Berko, 150-53. Tr. of 1981 French edition. Brussels: Editions Laconti, 1984.

Hunter, William Wilson. *A Statistical Account of Bengal.* 20 vols. London: Trubner, 1875-77.

Hutchinson, Robert Henry Sneyd. *Chittagong Hill Tracts.* Allahabad: Pioneer Press, 1909. Reprinted, Delhi: Virek, 1978.

India Office Library and Records. *Annual Report 1985-86.* London: British Library, 1987.

Jansen, Eirik G., et al. *The Country Boats of Bangladesh.* Dhaka: University Press, 1989.

Jansen, Eirik G. *Sailing Against the Wind: Boats and Boatmen of Bangladesh.*

Photographs by Trygve Bolstad. Dhaka: University Press Ltd., 1992.

Kattenhorn, Patricia. *British Drawings in the India Office Library*. Vol. 3. London: The British Library, 1995.

Kemp, Peter. *The Oxford Companion to Ships and the Sea*. Oxford: Oxford University Press, 1976.

———, and Richard Ormond. *The Great Age of Sail: Maritime Art and Photography*. Oxford: Phaidon, 1986.

Kerchove, René de. *International Maritime Dictionary*. New York: Van Norstrand, 1948.

Kindersley, Mrs. Nathaniel. *Letters from the Island of Tenerisse, Brazil, the Cape of Good Hope, and the East Indies*. London: J. Nourse, 1777.

Lawrence, Honoria. *The Journals of Honoria Lawrence: India Observed 1837-1854*. Edited by John Lawrence and Audrey Woodiwiss. London: Hodder & Stroughton, 1980.

Lewis, Ivor. *Sahibs, Nabobs, and Boxwallahs: A Dictionary of the Words of Anglo-India*. Bombay: Oxford University Press, 1991.

Long, Rev. James. *Calcutta in the Olden Time: Its Localities & Its People*. Calcutta: Sanskrit Pustak Bhandar, 1974. First published in *Calcutta Review* 18 (Dec. 1852): 275-320, and 35 (Sept. 1860):164-217.

Losty, J. P. "The Belgian Artists F. B. Solvyns and his Influence on Company Painting." *The British Libary, India Office Library and Records, Oriental Manuscripts and Printed Books Newsletter*. Nos. 37-38 (March 1987), 6-9.

MacGregor, David R. *The Schooner: Its Design and Development from 1600 to the Present*. Annapolis: Naval Institute Press, 1997.

Martin, Montgomery. *The History, Antiquities, Topography, and Statistics of Eastern India*. 4 vols. London: Wm. H. Allen, 1838. Principally a compilation of survey materials by Francis Buchanan.

Marshman, John Clark. "Notes on the Left or Calcutta Bank of the Hooghly" *Calcutta Review* 3 (January 1845). In *Calcutta Keepsake*, edited by Alok Ray, 181-82. Calcutta: Rddhi-India, 1978.

Milbourn, William. *Oriental Commerce*. New edition. London: Kingsbury, Parbury, and Allen, 1825. [First edition, 2 vols., London: 1813.]

Mukherjee, Nilmani. *The Port of Calcutta: A Short History*. Calcutta: Commissioners for the Port of Calcutta, 1968.

Mookerji, Radha Kumud. *Indian Shipping: A History of Seaborne Trade and Maritime Activity of the Indians from Earliest Times*. London: Longmans, Green and Co., 1912. Reprinted, Allahabad: Kitab Mahal, 1962.

Mundy, Captain G.C. *Pen and Pencil Sketches, Being a Journal of a Tour of India*. 2 vols. London: John Murray, 1832.

Nair, P. Thankappan, ed. *British Social Life in Ancient Calcutta (1750-1850)*. Calcutta: Sanskrit Pustak Bhandas, 1983.

———, ed. *Calcutta in the 18th Century*. Calcutta: Firma KLM, 1984.

———, ed. *Calcutta in the 19th Century*. Calcutta: Firma KLM, 1989.

Nandy, Somendra Chandra. *Life and Times of Cantoo Baboo: The Banian of Warren Hastings*. 2 vols. Vol. 1: Bombay: Allied, 1978; Vol. 2: Calcutta: Dev-All, 1981.

National Maritime Museum. *Concise Catalog of Oil Paintings in the National Maritime Museum*. Woodbridge, Suffolk: Antique Collector's Club, 1988.

Noel, John V. *The VNR Dictionary of Ships and the Sea*. New York: Van Nostrand Reinhold, 1981.

Nugent, Lady Maria. *A Journal From the Year 1811 till the Year 1815*. 2 vols. London: 1839.

Oriental Annual, The. London: Charles Tilt, 1837.

Parks, Fanny. *Wanderings of a Pilgrim, in Search of the Picturesque*. 2 vols. Karachi: Oxford University Press, 1975 [1850].

Popham, Hugh. *A Damned Cunning Fellow: The Eventful Life of Rear-Admiral Sir Home Popham, KCB, KCH, KM, FRS, 1762-1820*. Tywardreath, Cornwall: Old Ferry Press, 1991.

Prinsep, G.A. *An Account of Steam Vessels and of Proceedings Connected with Steam Navigation in British India*. Calcutta: Government Gazette Press, 1830.

Rahman, M. Akhlaqur. *The Country Boats of East Pakistan: An Economic Analysis*. Dhaka: East Pakistan Inland Water Transport Authority, 1963.

Ray, Alok, ed. *Calcutta Keepsake*. Calcutta: Rddhi-India, 1978.

Risley, Herbert H. *The Tribes and Castes of Bengal*. 2 vols. Calcutta: Bengal Secretariat Press, 1891.

Rizvi, S.N.H. *East Pakistan District Gazetteers: Chittagong*. Dacca: East Pakistan Government Press, 1970.

Roberts, Emma. *Scenes and Characteristics of Hindostan, with Sketches of Anglo-Indian Society*. 3 vols. London: W.H. Allen, 1835. 2nd ed., 2 vols. London: W.H. Allen, 1837.

Sen, Sukumar. *An Etymological Dictionary of Bengali: c. 1000-1800 A.D.* Calcutta: Eastern, 1971.

Seton-Karr, W.S., ed. *Selections from Calcutta Gazettes. . . . showing the political and social condition of he English in India*. Micrographic ed. 9 vols. Calcutta: Bibhash Gupta, 1987. Vol. 2 (1789-1792). Originally published Calcutta: Military Orphans Press, 1864-1869.

Sketches of India; or Observations Descriptive of the Scenery, &c, in Bengal. London: Black, Parbury, and Allen, 1816.

Sketches of India: Written by an Officer for Fire-side Travellers at Home. London: Longman et al., 1821.

Smith, Philip C.F. *More Marine Paintings and Drawings in the Peabody Museum*. Salem, MA: Peabody Museum, 1979.

Smyth, Adm. William Henry. *The Sailor's Word-Book: An Alphabetical Digest of Nautical Terms.* London: Blackie and Son, 1867.

Solvyns, François Balthazar [Baltazard]. *A Catalogue of 250 Coloured Etchings; Descriptive of the Manners, Customs, Character, Dress, and Religious Ceremonies of the Hindoos.* Calcutta: Mirror Press, 1799.

———. *A Collection of Two Hundred and Fifty Coloured Etchings: Descriptive of the Manners, Customs and Dresses of the Hindoos.* Calcutta, 1796, 1799.

———. *The Costume of Indoostan* [pirated edition]. London: Edward Orme, 1804, 1807.

———. *Les Hindoûs.* 4 vols. Paris: Chez L'Auteur, 1808-1812.

Spink & Son Ltd. *A Journey Through India: Pictures of India by British Artists.* [Catalogue for the sale of October 9-November 1, 1996.] London: Spink & Son, Ltd., 1996.

Stanhope, Philip Dormer ["Asiaticus"]. *Genuine Memoirs of Asiaticus.* 2d ed. Reprint by the Calcutta Historical Society. Introduction and notes by Walter Kelly Firminger. Hugli: L. Chowdhury, 1909 [1785].

Stavorinus, Johan Splinter. *Voyages to the East-Indies* [1768-71]. Translated from the Dutch by Samuel H. Wilcocke. 3 vols. London: G.G. and J. Robinson, 1798.

Stocqueler, J.H. [Joachim H. Siddons]. *The Hand-Book of India.* London: W.H. Allen, 1844.

———. *The Oriental Interpreter.* London: James Madden, 1848.

Sutton, Jean. *Lords of the East: The East India Company and its Ships.* London: Conway Maritime Press, 1981.

Tennant, Rev. William. *Indian Recreation; consisting chiefly of strictures on the domestic and rural economy of the Mohomedans & Hindoos,* 2nd ed., 3 vols. London: Longman, Hurst, Rees & Orwe, 1804-8.

Tripati, Sila. "Ports and Maritime Activities in Orissa (16th to 19th Centuries)." In *Ship-building and Navigation in the Indian Ocean, AD 1400-1800,* 155-64. New Delhi: Munshiram Manoharlal, 1997.

Valentia, Viscount George. *Voyages and Travels to India.* 4 vols. London: F.C., and J. Rivington, 1811.

Van Nouhuys, F.W. "The Anchor." *The Mariner's Mirror: The Journal of the Society for Nautical Research* (1951): 17-47.

Williamson, Captain Thomas. *The East India Vide-Mecum.* 2 vols. London: Black, Parry & Kingsbury, 1810. Digested by J.B. Gilchrist, 1825.

Wilson, Charles Robert, and W.H. Carey. *Glimpses of the Olden Times: India Under East India Company.* Edited by Amarendranath Mookerji. Calcutta: Eastlight Book House, 1968.

Woussen, Martine. "Frans Balthasar Solvyns." In *1770-1830: Autour du Neo-Classicisme en Belgique,* edited by Denis Coekelberghs and Pierre, 304. Brussels: Crédit Communal, 1985.

Yule, Henry, and A.C. Burnell. See *Hobson-Jobson.*